g. The book. The book remembers everything. The book remem
members everything. The book remembers ev
ything. The book remembers everything. The
ook remembers. The book remembers everythin
everything. The book remembers everything.
nembers everything. The book remembers everything. The book rem
. The book remembers everything. The book remembers everythin
nbers everything. The book. The book. The book remembers.
s everything. The book remembers everything. The book remem
The book remembers everything. The book remembers everything. The
ers everything. The book remembers. The book remembers. The book re
ng. The book remembers everything. The book. The book remembers eve
nembers everything. The book remembers everything. The book remem
everything. everything. The book remembers everything. The book re
ers everything. The book remembers everything. The book remem
The book remembers everything. The book remembers everything
members everything. The book remembers everything. The book

Nancy Kuhl

# THE BOOK REMEMBERS EVERYTHING

## THE WORK OF ERICA VAN HORN

Coracle | Granary Books 2010

Published with the generous assistance of William and Joan Roth and Michael Mann and Deborah Wexler.

Coracle
Ballybeg, Grange, Clonmel, Tipperary, Ireland
www.coracle.ie
ISBN 978–0–906630–41–9

Granary Books, Inc.
www.granarybooks.com
ISBN 978–1–887123–79–2


Editorial design by Simon Cutts
Layout design by Colin Sackett
Printed and bound in China

Distributed in the U.K. and Europe by
Cornerhouse Publications
70 Oxford Street, Manchester M1 5NH
www.cornerhouse.org

Distributed to the trade in the U.S.A. by
D.A.P./Distributed Art Publishers
155 Avenue of the Americas, New York, NY 10013
Orders: (800) 338–2665
www.artbook.com

Also available from
Small Press Distribution
1341 Seventh Street, Berkeley, CA 94710
Orders: (800) 869–7553
www.spdbooks.org

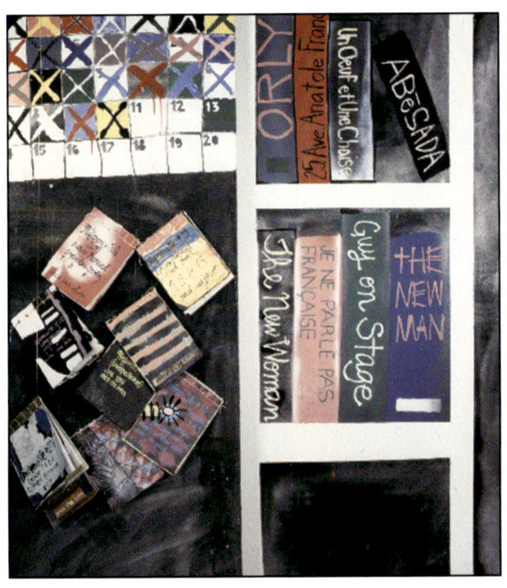
ORLY
25 Ave Anatole Fran
Un Oeuf et Une Chaise
The New Woman
JE NE PARLE PAS FRANÇAISE
Guy on Stage
THE NEW MAN

I've been making books since the day President Kennedy was shot. That day I was in the 4th grade in Pittsfield, NH. As we lined up on the stairs to go home, my teacher, Mrs.Tuttle, was weeping. We all found this very funny. Later, my parents' shock and attention made me realize something Big had happened. I went to the front room and began to work. The TV stayed on all the next day. We all watched and listened and tried to understand. I ran back and forth from my table in the front room to the TV. I made detailed reports of each developement. I drew all the pictures.

My great-grandmother died that day. My sister, Stephanie, and I were convinced that she died just because President Kennedy was getting all the attention. She was a selfish woman. She married her first cousin so she wouldn't have to change her monogram. I've always meant to do a book about her.
Later, my mother showed me how to sew the pages of my Kennedy Bookings together into a book. A few years afterward, Stephanie found the book in a drawer of Mum's desk. She teased me about the stupid text and the stupid drawings, so I tore it up. ~~My mother wept.~~

That made my mother cry.

*Preface to an exhibition at Franklin Furnace, New York 1986*

# INTRO-DUCTION

In the work of Erica Van Horn, books collect and transform remnants, remembrances, and reminders. From fragments that might otherwise be forgotten, the artist makes new meanings in beautiful and unexpected ways. "I use the portability of the printed sheet, mostly in book form," she writes, "to construct a narrative around the incidental parts of my life."

Van Horn weaves together her methods and preoccupations into the common fabric of her work. Her interest in exploring the daily aspects of her life though art, for instance, is informed and determined by her frequent use and re-use of ordinary materials as the principal elements of her work. A creative tension is always present between her interest in language as a practical and physical matter worthy of sustained exploration and her deep interest in visual narrative; textual and imagistic qualities of identity, community, and memory are revealed by contrast and comparison.

*The Book Remembers Everything* developed as a result of a 2010 exhibition of the outstanding collection of Erica Van Horn's work in the Yale Collection of American Literature at the Beinecke Rare Book and Manuscript Library at Yale University, including early works on paper, elaborately illustrated unique books, and printed and editioned works in a wide variety of formats. Like the exhibition, this book represents aspects of the artist's development over more than thirty years, exploring common elements throughout the extensive body of her work; it also extends the work of the exhibition by including new books and collaborations from Van Horn's recent work and additional examples of unique bookworks from early periods.

It is evident from the artist's early print and collage work that many characteristics of both her practice and her primary thematic concerns were present from the beginning. As a young artist and print maker, Van Horn used *chine-collé*, a method that allows for the addition of collage elements during the printing process, to incorporate unique pieces into each of the prints in an edition: "Since all of my collage elements were found and saved things," she has written, "every print became a unique object as the collage elements changed each time… I used the prints as storage for remembering things."

Like her early prints, much of the artist's later work explores the documentation of daily events, the re-use of materials, the role of narrative in visual art, and the various and complex workings of memory. A chronological bibliographic checklist of works featured in *The Book Remembers Everything* makes visible both the artist's persistent attention to her subjects and the development of her creative process over time. Across her large body of work, it is possible to trace the progression of Van Horn's ideas and methods, including an interest in combining image and text in unusual ways and the evolution of the practice of incorporating documents and found textual objects into her work, from chine collé prints to later hand-finished, editioned book works.

To highlight these and other elements, *The Book Remembers Everything* organizes the work under the following six headings:

DAILY DETAIL examines the frequent exploration of the elements of her life, the objects around her, the singular routine of her days, and her most familiar relationships.

WORDS FOR LIVING LOCALLY illustrates the artist's long fascination with the ways language both describes and creates community, even as it determines individual identity and shapes personal memory.

LEFTOVERS celebrates the artist's frequent use and re-use of saved or salvaged materials as the raw materials of her work, documenting the process of making meaning from fragments and remainders.

WORLD OF INTERIORS documents a years-long, large-scale project exposing and reusing the printed interiors of paper envelopes in works that question the role of beauty in a world of disposable objects and elevate the work of the collector into the realm of fine art.

NARRATIVE AND PATTERN reveals the interest in the essential elements of narrative forms, in both word and image, and the investigation of narrative structures by paring stories down to simple elements or couching them in rich landscapes of visual information.

IDENTITY AND LIKENESS emphasizes the frequent use of unconventional modes of portraiture to make visual and textual likenesses of people and places, exploring the visual nature of memory and the relationship between image and identity.

*The Book Remembers Everything* insists that the book is to be valued as a record of an event, a landscape, a creative vision, an obsession, or the most quotidian of activities, even if the book revises or re-imagines that which it documents. Erica Van Horn's books discover, explore, and sometimes enact their specific content; each tells the story of its making, its reason for being, and its author's process.

# DAILY DETAIL

Erica Van Horn regularly draws the subject of her work directly from the fabric of her daily life, her domestic and artistic work, the simple household objects at hand, the day-to-day aspects of familiar relationships. Art based on (and sometimes incorporating) modest, everyday things locates aesthetic qualities in the most immediate world around both artist and audience. Elevating simple objects and daily traditions to the world of fine art demonstrates the importance of honoring and commemorating that which might otherwise be forgotten or overlooked. Her focused attention on the *everyday* creates work that serves as an aid to memory and acts as a foil to the inevitable passing of one day to the next. Her work is a kind of talisman against the eventual end of a ritual, a place, a relationship, a person. In remembering and making beautiful the mundane aspects of life, the artist celebrates the significant but often unnoticed habits and customs of family and friendship, the exquisite qualities of home, the work of making art.

**Rusted**

Coracle, 2004

*Rusted* exemplifies an interest in the unassuming articles and quotidian practices of daily work, be it domestic labor in and around her home and the surrounding land or in the work of making art. The first page of *Rusted* describes the images that follow: "six small iron articles of unknown use found & drawn." Describing the work in greater detail, the artist writes: "Over the last ten years, I have found these metal implements: sprockets, chisels, cotter pins, mostly things for which I don't have names. They appear regularly in the soil of this former farm in Tipperary. Each metal piece was a part of something, a solution to a specific problem. That is all I know. I draw them in this simple silhouette form so that I will not forget them."

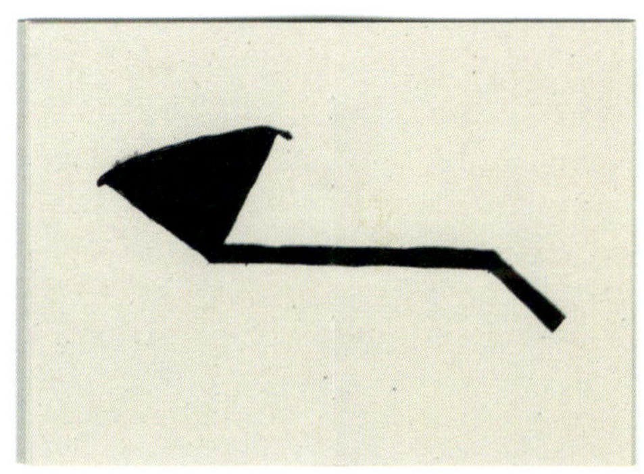

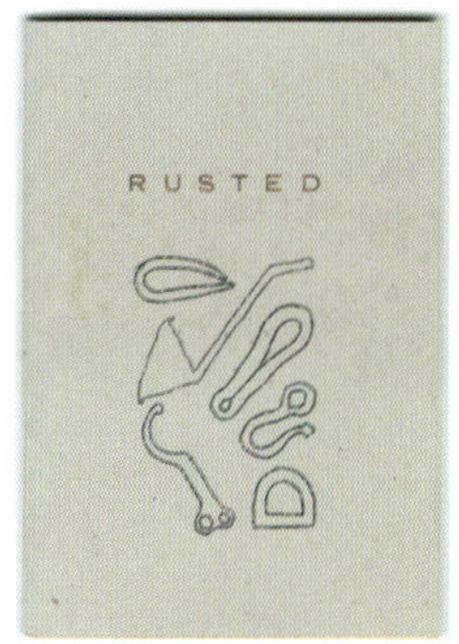

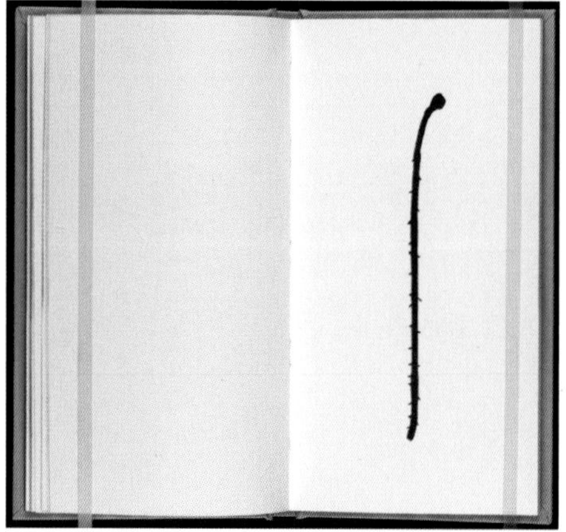

**14 Blackthorns: a Fascicule**

with Simon Cutts, Coracle, 1999

Combining silhouette images with poetry by her husband and frequent collaborator, the artist and poet Simon Cutts, *14 Blackthorns* documents their discovery of a bundle of blackthorn walking sticks in the barn on their property in rural Tipperary, Ireland: "a bundle found / in the soft floor / of the barn / tied with baling / twine & bound / for market." In a simple form the book incorporates a complex series of associations: the artists acknowledge the history of their home and workspace—once a barn, the building now functions as an artist's studio—and highlight the value of the different kinds of work that has taken place there; making artwork based on blackthorn walking sticks, like shillelaghs, a common symbol of Irishness, the expatriate artists also honor their adopted home country. The 'fascicule' of the title refers to the bundle of sticks, but as the term also names part of a work published in installments, it points to Van Horn's return to the subject of blackthorns in other printed formats, including prints and ephemeral publications.

**A Few Cups**

Coracle, 2007

This group of prints provides an example of the value the artist finds in the forms of objects encountered in daily life and her ability to focus careful attention on even the most familiar things. Printed in deep Prussian blue ink, the nine prints depict the shapes and surfaces of simple cups. Like the drawings in *14 Blackthorns*, the work is a study in repetition and variation, and in the pleasure of locating subtle differences in similar objects.

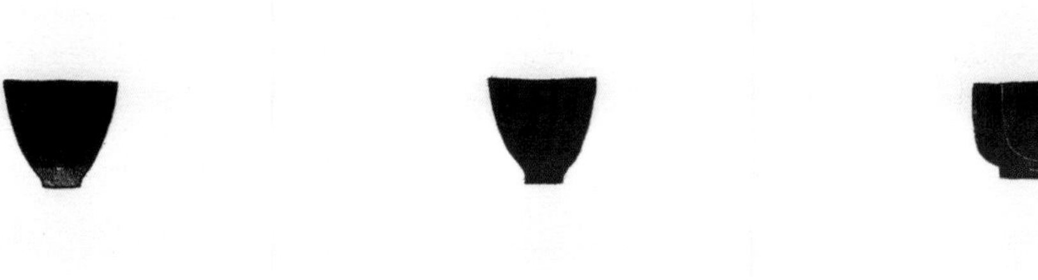

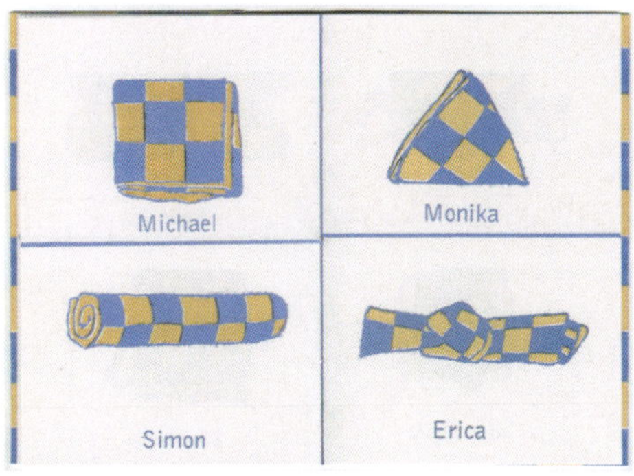


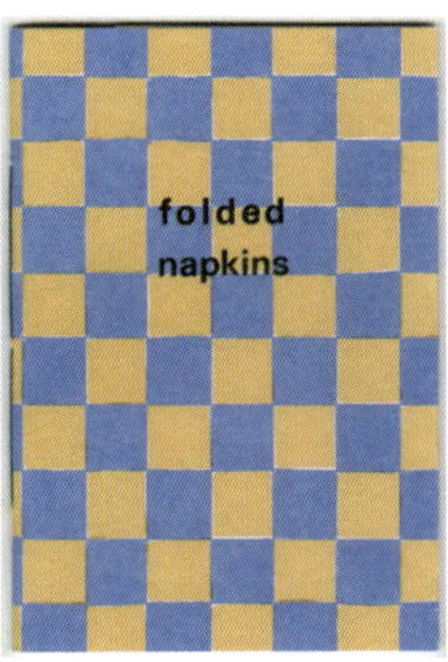


## Folded Napkins

Coracle, 2006

This book documents a collection of drawings made over time with a specific purpose in mind: "When we have guests staying for a few days, I ask them to fold their napkins in a particular way so that they will remember which one is theirs. Sometimes they remember and sometimes they forget, so I often make a drawing." If the book provides a whimsical record of visitors, it also obliquely highlights the importance of breaking bread with friends. In documenting this tradition, the artist considers domestic behavior and tradition reflected in the personalization of social customs.

### Aglio 6 Olio

with Simon Cutts, Coracle, 1992

Van Horn and Cutts refer to this little book as "an abstract cookbook whose structure emulates that of a symmetrical head of garlic. Each of the six cloves, each a section of the whole book, presents a recipe for one of the classic sauces of garlic and oil, plus one (or at the most two) other ingredients: aioli ... persillade ... pistou ... salsa ... rouille ... anchoïade." This 'garlic book,' and specifically Van Horn's drawings of the modest form of heads and cloves of garlic, call to mind the simple but powerful nature of food to unite people not only across a table but also across very different cultures.

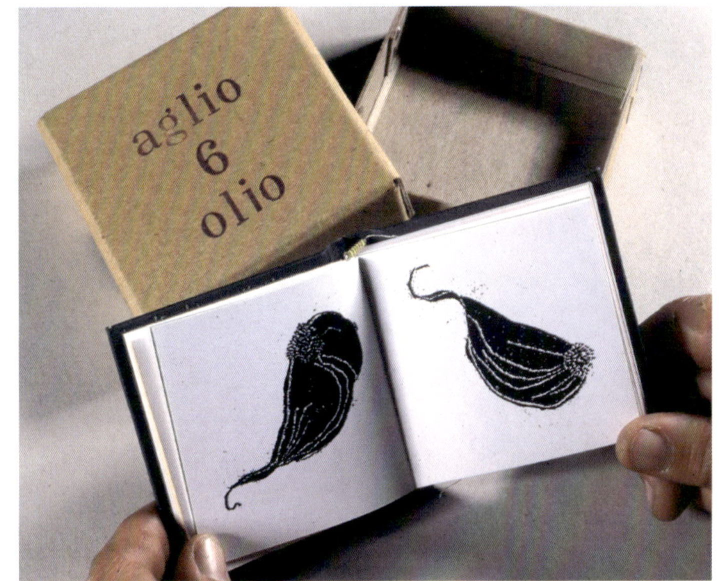

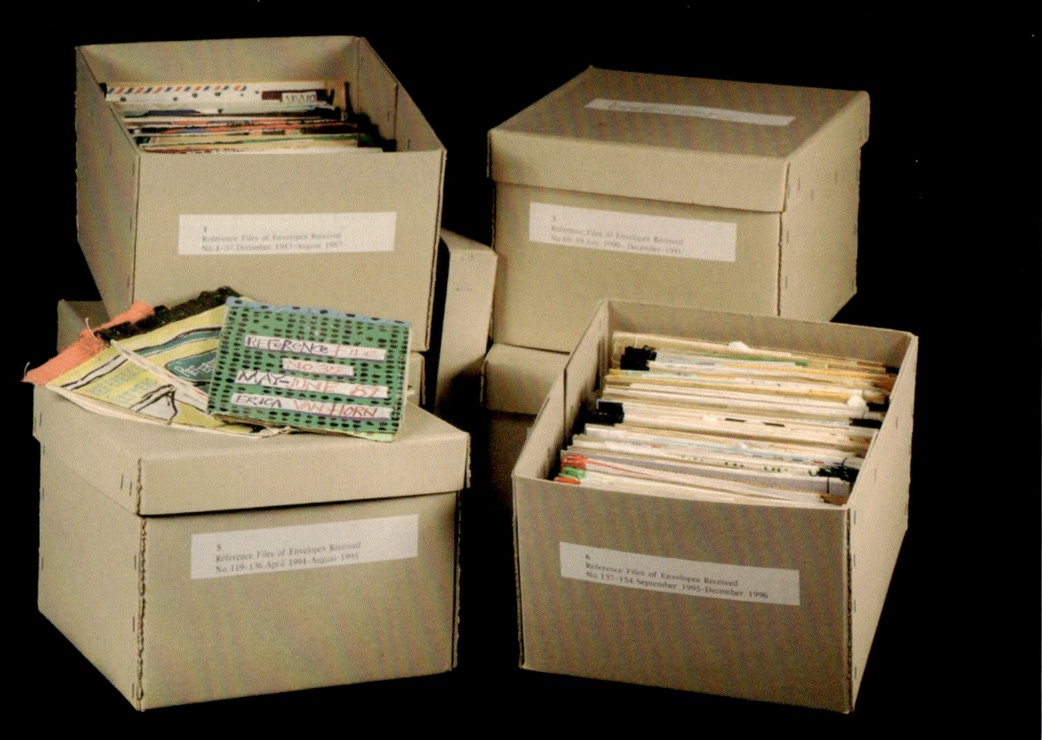
REFERENCE FILE
MAY-JUNE 87
ERICA VAN HORN
5
Reference Files of Envelopes Received
No.119-136 April 1994-August 1995
6
Reference Files of Envelopes Received
No.137-154 September 1995-December 1996

**Reference Files of Envelopes Received**

December 1983–December 1996

This singular work includes some 3,500 envelopes sewn into 154 books, housed in six large boxes. The envelopes are all addressed to Van Horn, or to her and her husband, at locations in the United States, England, France, and Italy, over a period of more than ten years. After keeping all her incoming correspondence for many years, the artist decided to discard the envelopes in an effort to pare down her possessions: "I decided the envelopes were dead weight. After sorting through and separating a few years worth, I felt very sad. The envelopes were a record of where I had been at moments during a peripatetic time. My solution was to sew them together in monthly batches." The resulting work is an exploration of memory, its fragmentary nature, its insistence, and its repetitions. Transforming the postmarked envelopes into something new both records their original meaning (a communication with a particular person, at a particular time, in a particular place) and creates a new and separate meaning for each envelope, now the component parts of a large-scale project.

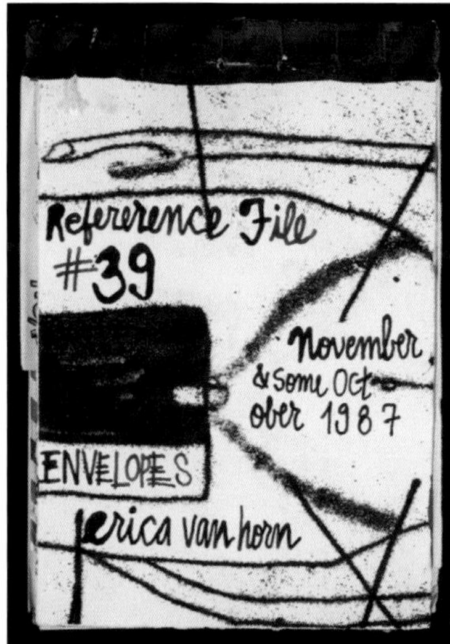

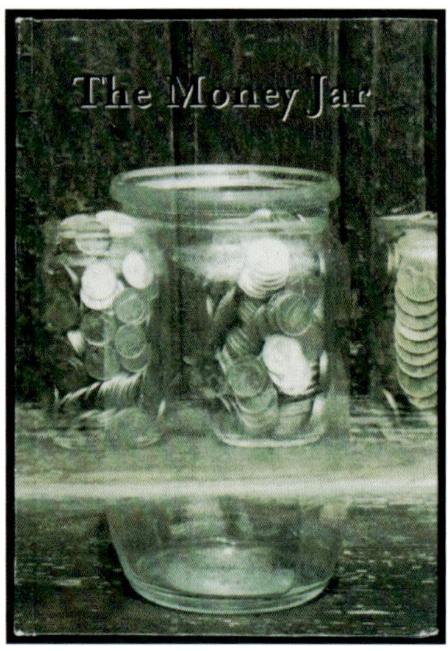


**The Money Jar**

with Simon Cutts, Coracle, 2002

Marking the withdrawal of Irish currency in favor of the Euro, this collaboration documents the habit of saving loose change in one-pound jars in a series of photographs and figures: "From 1.30am on Tuesday January 1st 2002, Irish currency will start to be withdrawn from circulation. At midnight on Saturday February 9th, it will cease to exist." The replacement of one currency with another, they suggest, represents a significant cultural shift, but because few materials are more common than coins, it is a change that is likely to be quickly forgotten. "This book" they write, "is not only a way of ending our collecting [Irish coins] but one of marking their ending."

### Stiles & the Pennine Way

Coracle, 1993

An unusual daily travel journal, *Stiles & the Pennine Way* records an eleven-day-long walking trip in England; seven days of the trip were spent walking the Pennine Way, a trail across the Pennines, a range of hills in the north of England. To keep from getting bored and as a way to distract herself from the steady rain, Van Horn kept track of the stiles she passed through or over during the walk by making hash marks on the sleeve of her raincoat with a waterproof pen. "I was very tidy about my little group of tally marks" she writes of her second day on the trail, "and found myself admiring my sleeve a lot through the afternoon, especially since it was raining hard and I had to keep my head down." Though the book includes a prose narrative about the trip, the drawing of the marked-up sleeves interrupts the text in its center, suggesting that the marks and the practice of making them are at least as important as the straightforward description of the journey.

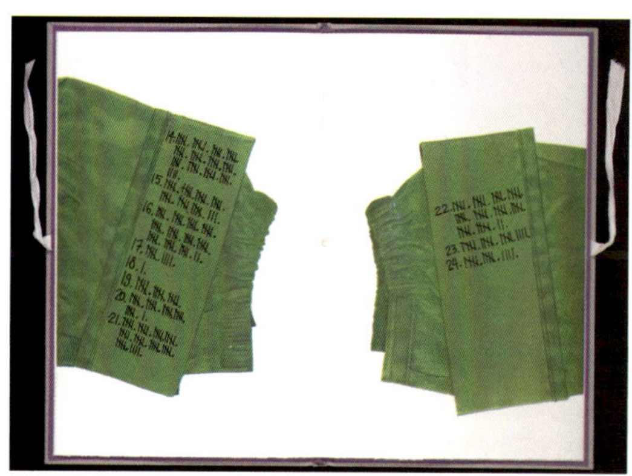

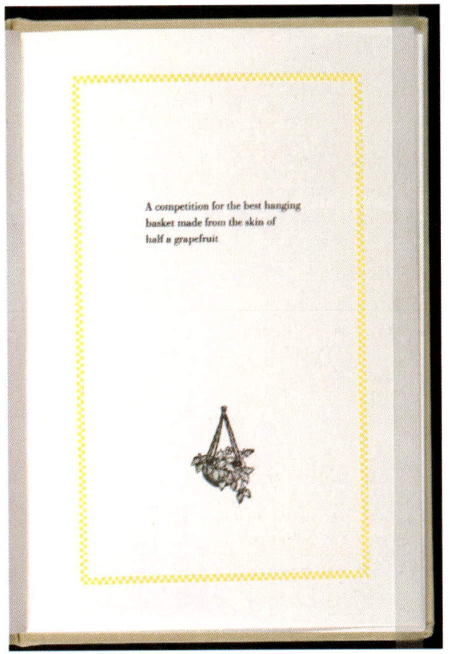


**Docking Competitions, 1991–95**
with Laurie Clark, Coracle, 1995

This collaboration sympathetically records four years worth of fund-raising competitions sponsored by the Docking chapters of the Women's Section of the Royal British Legion and the Women's Institute, two leading volunteer service organizations in Britain. The contests focus variously on household articles, craft projects, and gardening achievements, including awards for the prettiest hanky, the best hanging basket made from half a grapefruit, and the longest stick of rhubarb. By documenting the charitable work of these organizations using only the given descriptions of their contests accompanied by simple illustrations, the artists create a clever window on their community. The portrait that results finds humour in the tradition of such competitions with no sense of ridicule or mean-spiritedness.

**I Restrict Myself to Eight Favorite Things a Day**
Paris, 1983

Van Horn refers to this as a copybook for recording beloved things, a collection, the artist writes, of what "I was seeing as I went out and about everyday in France. Each day had one page which served as a title page, showing the day of the week. The grouping of nine could exist on the wall, or back in their folder as reference material."

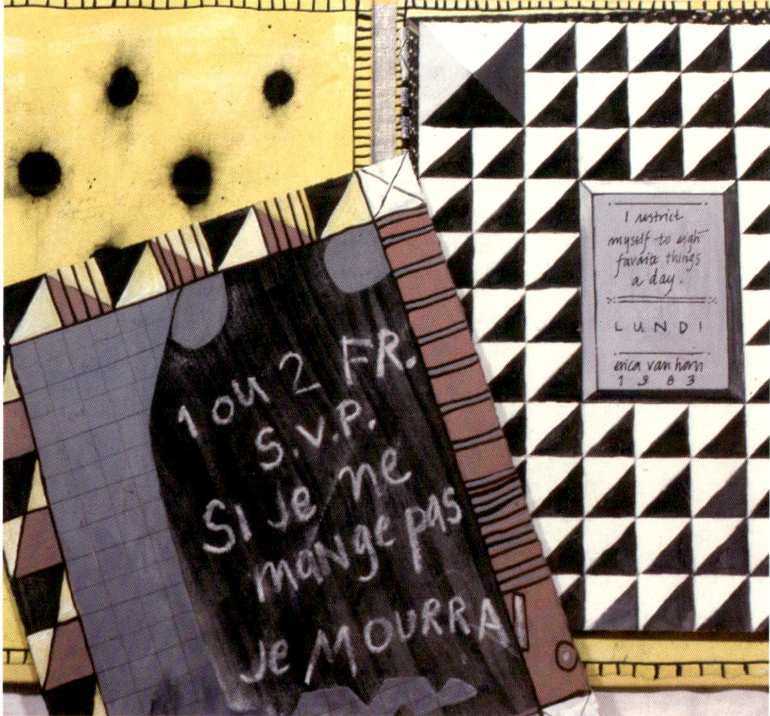

# WORDS FOR LIVING LOCALLY

Among the recurring themes that unite Erica Van Horn's diverse body of work through time, format, and material, is her fascination with language and its power to shape thought, experience, and memory. Exploring the relationship between language and place, the artist has considered *foreign* language and the site-specific *local* language of particular communities. While her focus is often on meaning, she never loses sight of the visual qualities of language, the ways in which handwriting and printing can inform our reading of both public and private documents. Living for extended periods in France and Italy, she has explored the languages of these places in text and image, narrative and abstraction, exposing much about their culture, landscape, and character. This work also questions the ways language can mark one as a foreigner, an outsider in a linguistically defined community. As a long-term resident first of England and now of Ireland, countries whose residents share her native language, Van Horn is no less interested in the sometimes subtle and sometimes obvious differences she finds in varieties of English. In colloquialisms and regional language use, she identifies subtle truths about the ways language both describes and creates community. Work in this category also recognizes the deeply personal qualities of language and the significant part it plays in determining identity and experience, in making and understanding memory.

## Italian Lessons 1–17

Coracle, 1990–1997

Employing a wide variety of printed formats, from small books to postcards and even a commercially printed eraser, the *Italian Lessons* series explores language learning, the experience of living in a foreign country, and the relationship of language to place. The series of 'lessons' makes use of narrative, humor, nostalgia, image, and rhetoric to demonstrate a small fraction of the ways one encounters and experiences a foreign language. The *Lessons* also serve to document her time spent in Italy and they record not only the artist's attempts to learn a new language but also something of her daily experiences. From the process of making No. 13 in the series, Van Horn salvaged materials for the remnant book *I Fingerprinted Italian Lesson No.13*.

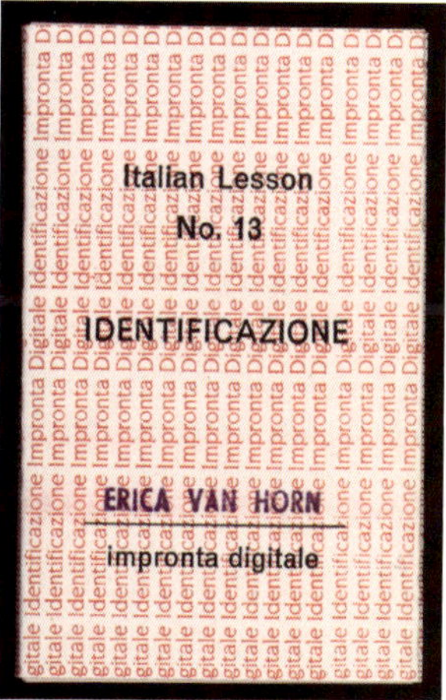


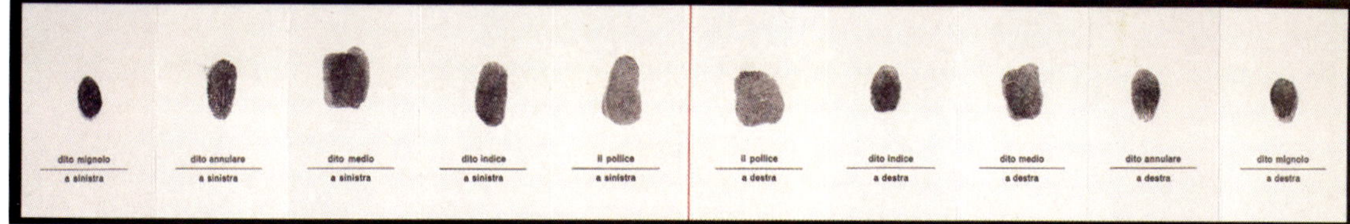

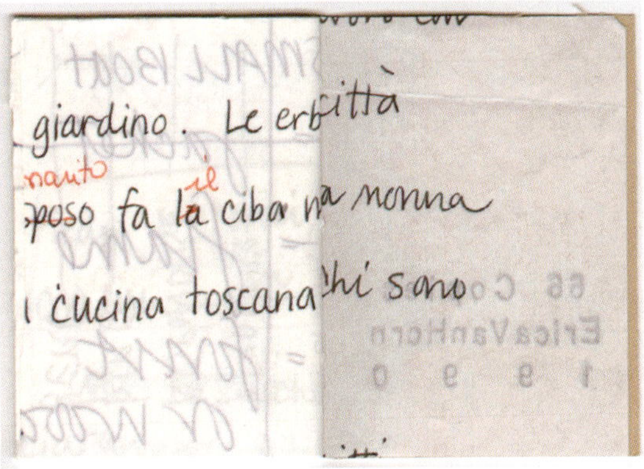

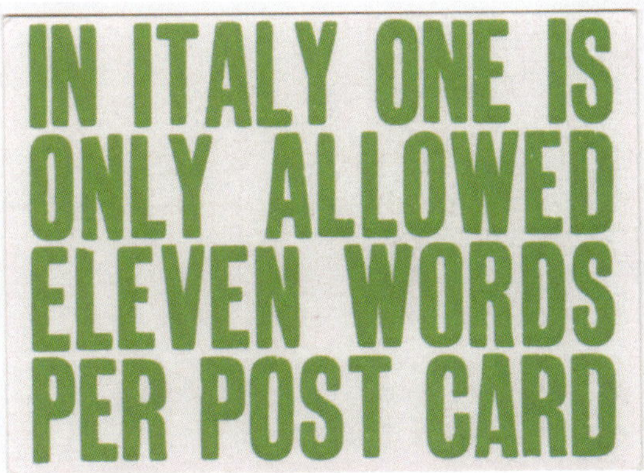

IN ITALY ONE IS
ONLY ALLOWED
ELEVEN WORDS
PER POST CARD

Italian Lessons Nos. 4 and 11

*Italian Lessons Nos. 8, 9, 10 and 17*

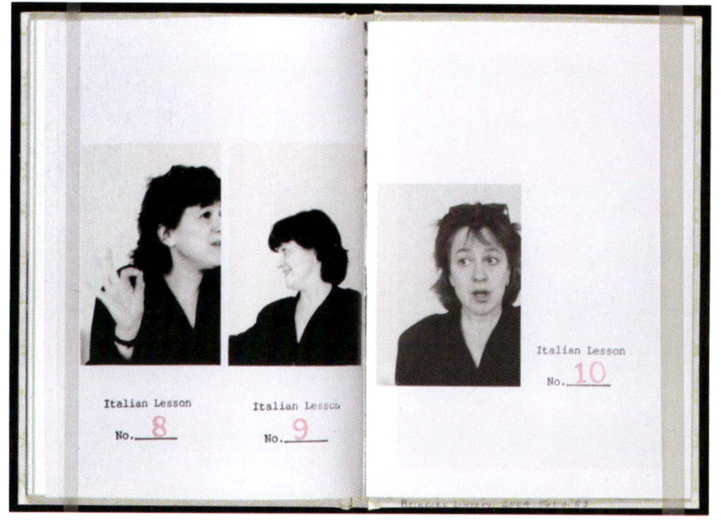


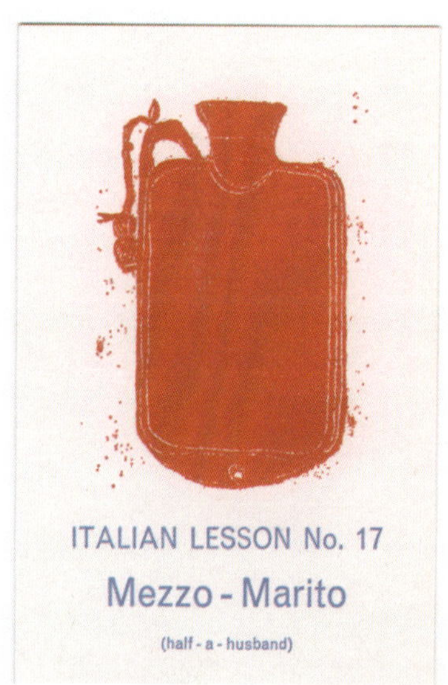

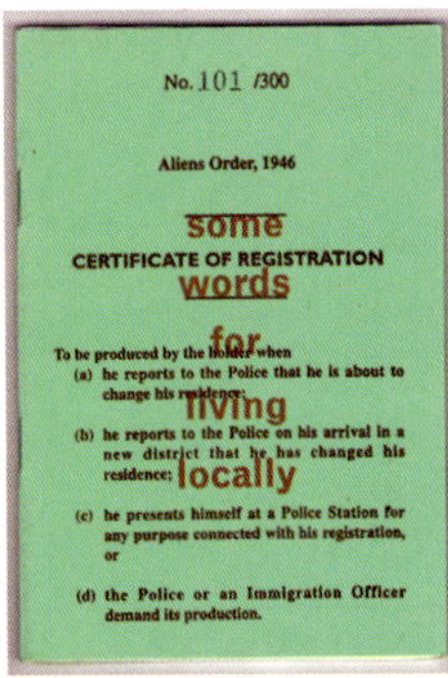
No. 101 /300

Aliens Order, 1946

some

CERTIFICATE OF REGISTRATION

words

for

living

locally

To be produced by the holder when
(a) he reports to the Police that he is about to change his residence;
(b) he reports to the Police on his arrival in a new district that he has changed his residence;
(c) he presents himself at a Police Station for any purpose connected with his registration, or
(d) the Police or an Immigration Officer demand its production.

## Living Locally 1–16

Coracle 2001–

The *Living Locally* series celebrates the landscape, culture, and community of Van Horn's adopted home in rural Tipperary, Ireland. Collecting, documenting, and illustrating the language of the region, she both acknowledges her position as a kind of outsider (a 'blow in', in the local slang, refers "to anyone who moves here from somewhere else") and locates herself firmly within the community. The *Living Locally* series calls attention to her sheer love of the curious and quirky turns she finds in English, the aurally pleasing sound combinations, the paradoxically conflicting meanings from one locale to another, and the language's endless flexibility and transformability.

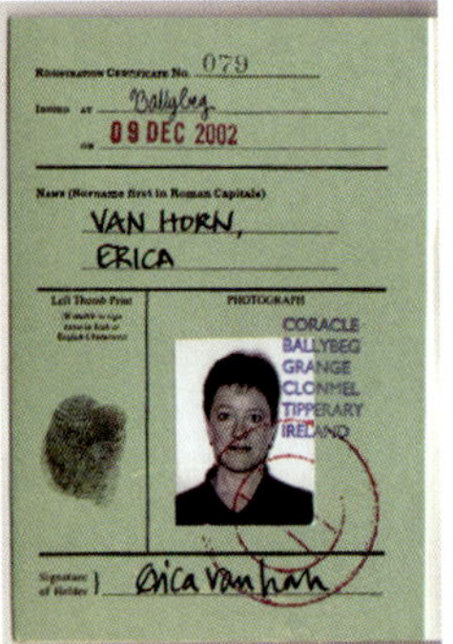
Registration Certificate No. 079

Issued at Ballybeg

on 09 DEC 2002

Name (Surname first in Roman Capitals) VAN HORN, ERICA

Left Thumb Print

PHOTOGRAPH

CORACLE
BALLYBEG
GRANGE
CLONMEL
TIPPERARY
IRELAND

Signature of Holder Erica Van Horn

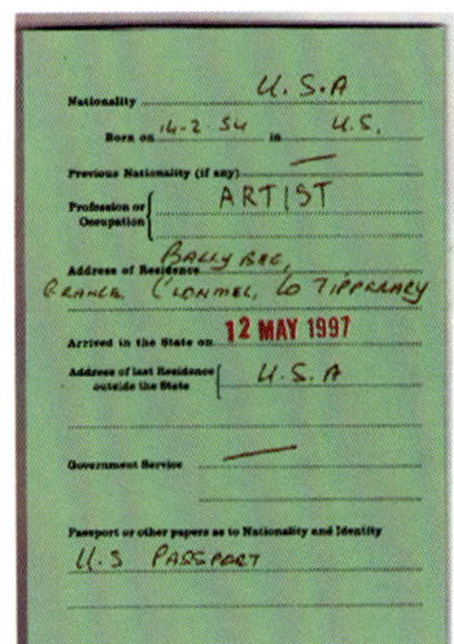
Nationality U.S.A

Born on 14-2-54 in U.S.

Previous Nationality (if any) —

Profession or Occupation ARTIST

Address of Residence Ballybeg, Grange, Clonmel, Co Tipperary

Arrived in the State on 12 MAY 1997

Address of last Residence outside the State U.S.A

Government Service —

Passport or other papers as to Nationality and Identity U.S Passport

Some *Words for Living Locally* Nos. 1–8

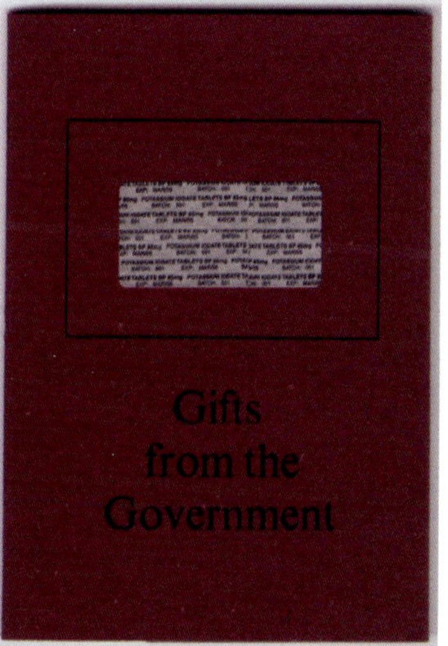


DEPARTMENT OF HEALTH AND CHILDREN
DUBLIN 2

POTASSIUM IODATE TABLETS BP 85mg

FOR USE AT THE TIME OF A NUCLEAR EMERGENCY

**What is in these tablets?**
The active ingredient in these tablets is potassium iodate. Each tablet contains 85mg of potassium iodate equivalent to 50mg of stable iodine. Also contains: Dicalcium Phosphate, Microcrystalline Cellulose, Silica, Stearic Acid, Sodium Croscarmellose, Magnesium Stearate.
Tablet coating: Hydroxypropylmethylcellulose Glycerine.
Each pack contains 6 tablets.

**How do these tablets work in the event of a nuclear accident?**
These tablets work by 'topping up' the thyroid gland with stable iodine in order to prevent it from accumulating any radioactive iodine that may have been released into the environment.

**Who has made these tablets?**
The tablets have been manufactured to the order of the Minister for Health and Children by a licensed manufacturer of medicinal products.

**What population groups are most likely to benefit from taking these tablets?**
These are:-
• Pregnant women;
• Women who are breast feeding;
• New-born infants;
• Infants, children and adolescents up to the age of 18 years.
Priority should be given to these groups as the benefit to other population groups is limited.

**Are there persons who should not take these tablets?**
The only people who should not take these tablets are those who know that they are allergic to iodine and those who suffer from the very rare conditions of hypocomplementaemic vasculitis or dermatitis herpetiformis. Your doctor will have told you if you suffer from any of these conditions.

O K To Accept
Subject Checking

POTASSIUM IODATE TABLETS BP 85mg
CONTENTS: 6 TABLETS

FOR EMERGENCY USE ONLY IN THE EVENT OF A NUCLEAR ACCIDENT

During the months of June and July 2002, a packet containing six Potassium Iodate tablets BP 85 mg was delivered to households throughout the country as part of the National Emergency Plan for Nuclear Accidents. Our tablets expired in 2005. There has never been any further mention of these tablets, nor of a potential accident.

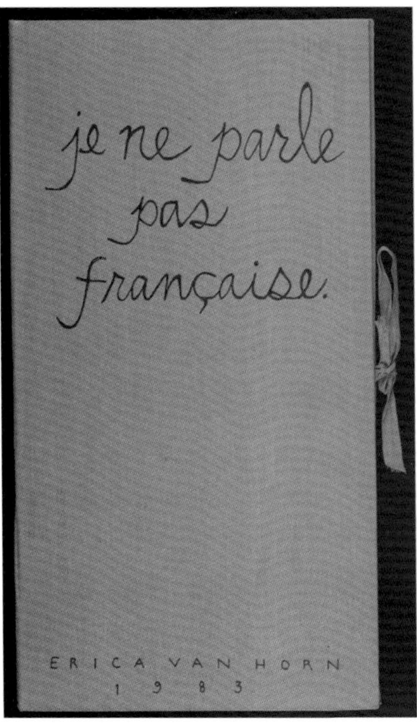


**Je Ne Parle Pas Francaise**

Paris 1983

Years before beginning the *Italian Lessons* series, Van Horn made several books documenting her experience learning French while living in Paris. Part book, part board game, *Je Ne Parle Pas Francaise*, or *I do not speak French*, plays with the relationship between image and text, 'illustrating' various verbs with simple drawings that combine personal associations with the words' standard meanings. The choice of particular verbs—including activities, as in 'to eat' and 'to drink', verbs focusing on the visual, such as 'to see' and 'to look at', and others describing more emotional states, like 'to be afraid' and 'to amuse'—suggests a kind of narrative of the artist's experience of the time and place of the work's creation. The intentional or accidental misspelling of the word 'francaise' calls attention to the difficult process of learning a new language.

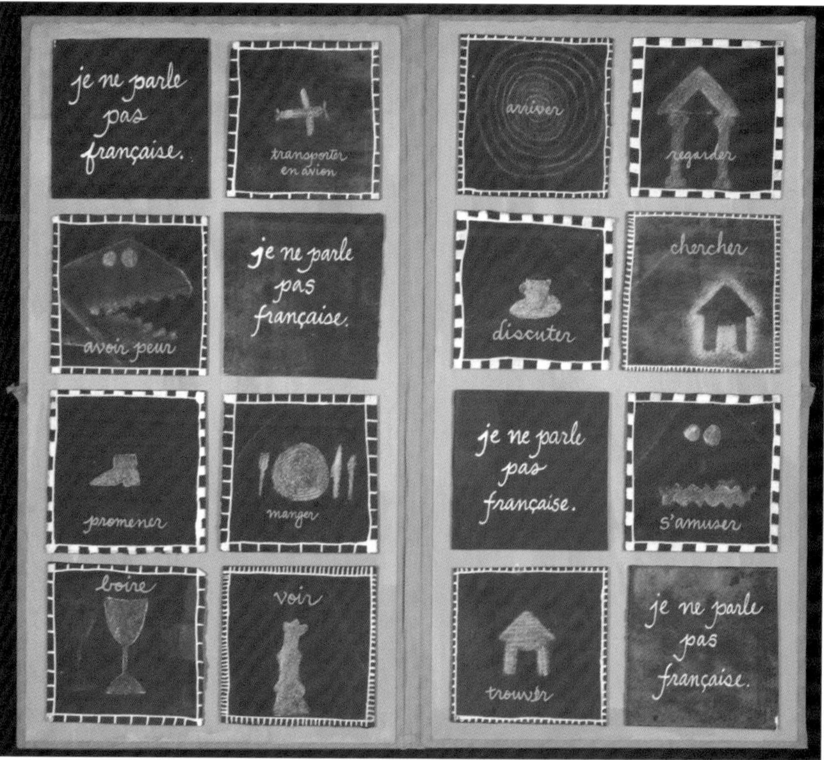

je ne parle
pas
française.
transporter
en avion
arriver
regarder
avoir peur
je ne parle
pas
française.
discuter
chercher
promener
manger
je ne parle
pas
française.
s'amuser
boire
voir
trouver
je ne parle
pas
française.

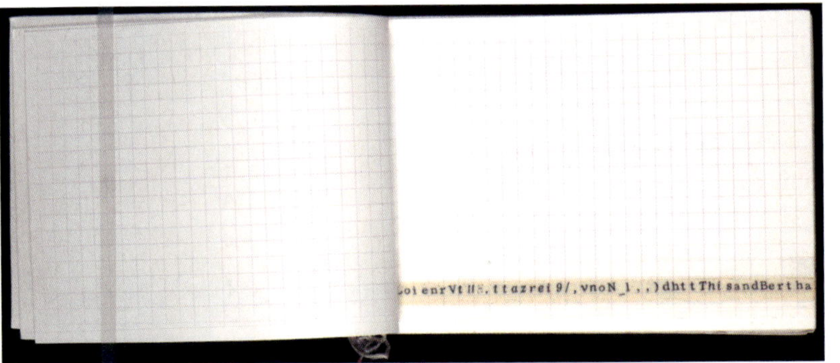

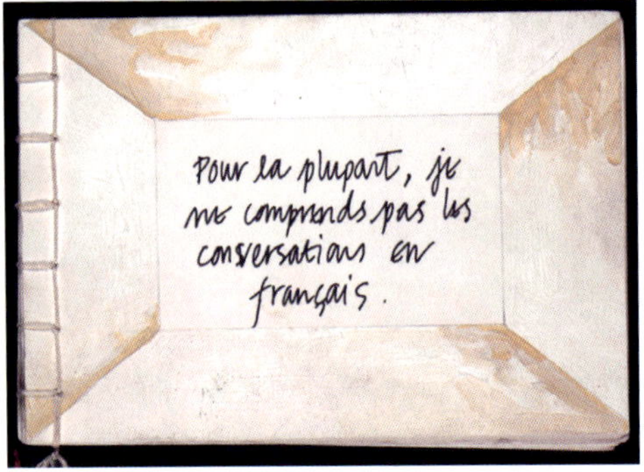


**Pour la plupart, Je ne comprends pas les conversations en français**
Vitry-sur-Seine, France 1983

...or 'For the most part, I don't understand conversations in French', is made up of unusual materials, including graphed board and typewriter correction tape. "The random letters look like gobbledy-gook" Van Horn writes, "a version of my frustration while listening to French."

## 25 Avenue Anatole France and the Neighborhood

Vitry-sur-Seine, France, 1984

In this narrative description of her community, Van Horn identifies her neighbors by their work: among others, readers encounter 'Monsieur et Madame Tabac, Monsieur le Boucher,' and 'Madame Post Office'. She complicates and enriches simple visual portrayals by providing brief but detailed descriptions of her observations and personal interactions: the tobacco shopkeepers "sell loto tickets with a seriousness befitting diamonds"; the butcher watches the Tour de France riders approach "on television through his living room window while [standing outside] on the sidewalk"; and of Madame Post Office, she writes, "we hate each other's guts". The artist combines elements of French and her native English to highlight ways she is and is not part of the community she describes; as an outside observer and current resident at once, she both documents and imaginatively illustrates her immediate surroundings.

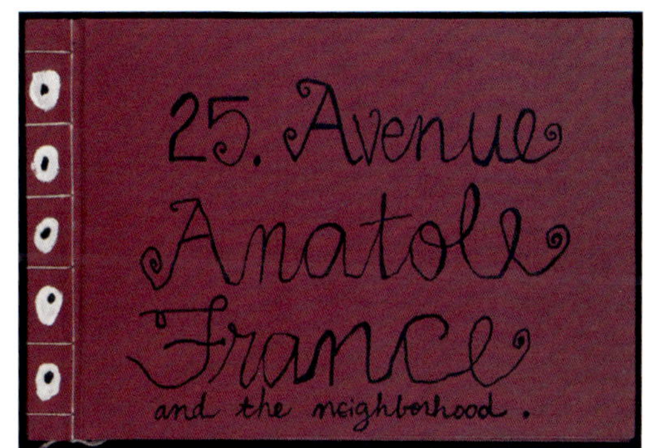

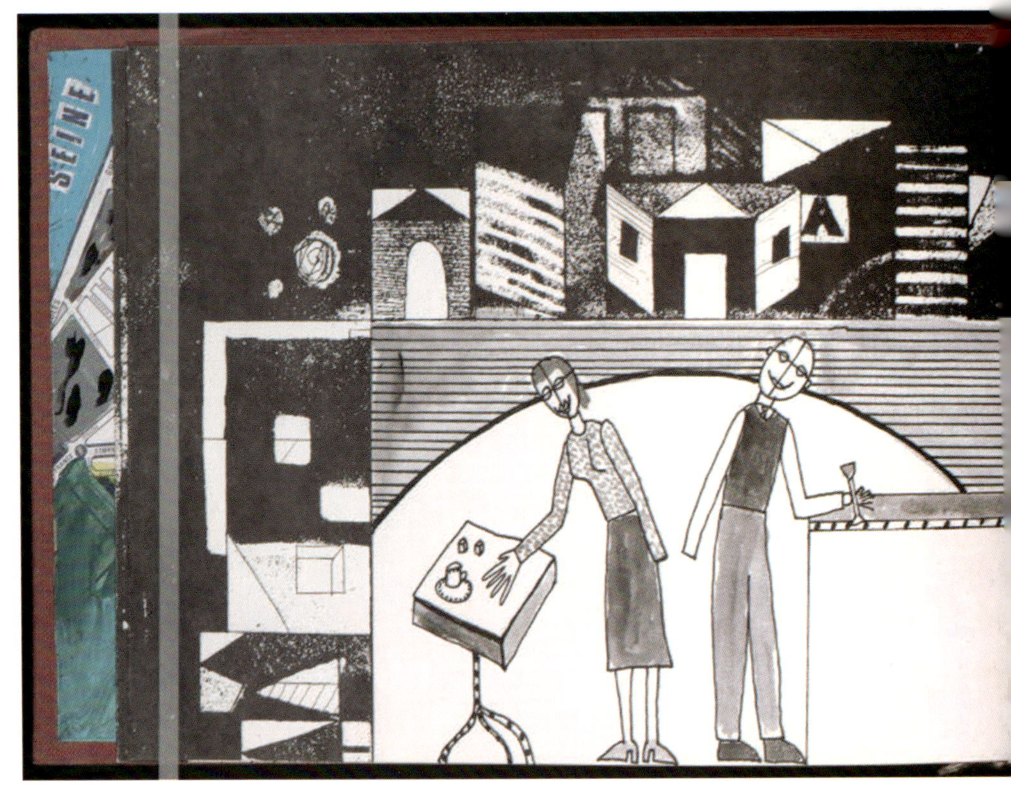
SEINE
A

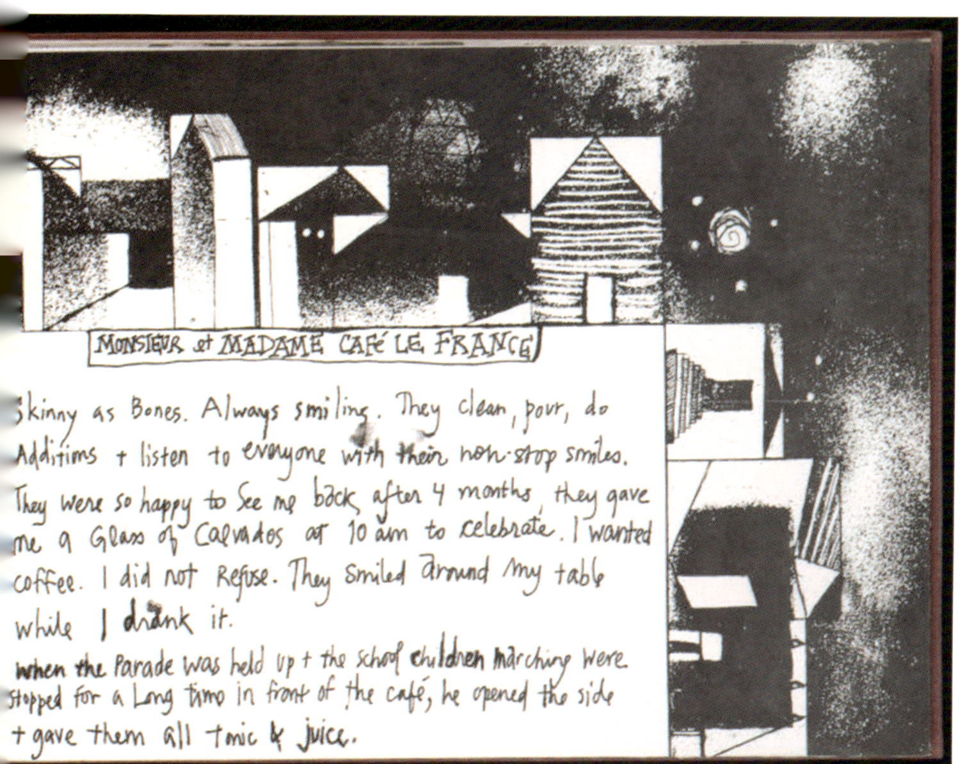
MONSIEUR et MADAME CAFÉ LE FRANCE
Skinny as Bones. Always smiling. They clean, pour, do Additims + listen to everyone with their non-stop smiles. They were so happy to See me back after 4 months, they gave me a Glass of Calvados at 10 am to celebrate. I wanted coffee. I did not Refuse. They smiled around my tabl while I drank it.
When the Parade was held up + the school children marching were stopped for a Long time in front of the café, he opened the side + gave them all tonic & juice.

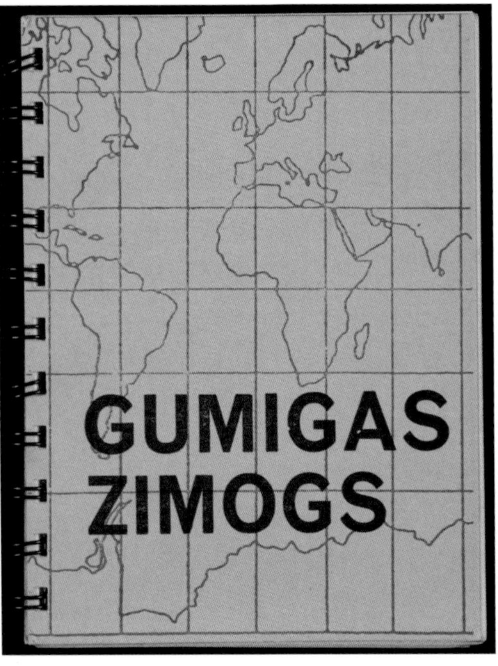


**Gumigas Zimogs: A World Guide to Rubber Stamps**
Coracle, 1996

Using various font styles and colors, this world guide to rubber stamps includes the words 'rubber stamp' individually stamped in numerous languages, representing countries around the world. The book, an obvious celebration of this utilitarian printing technology, also exhibits the words as a collection, extending the artist's interest in assembling groups of similar things to include language. In this way, the album demonstrates her interest in language as a material. Test sheets for this work were re-used in *Remnant Book of Practice Pages for Gumigas Zimogs*.

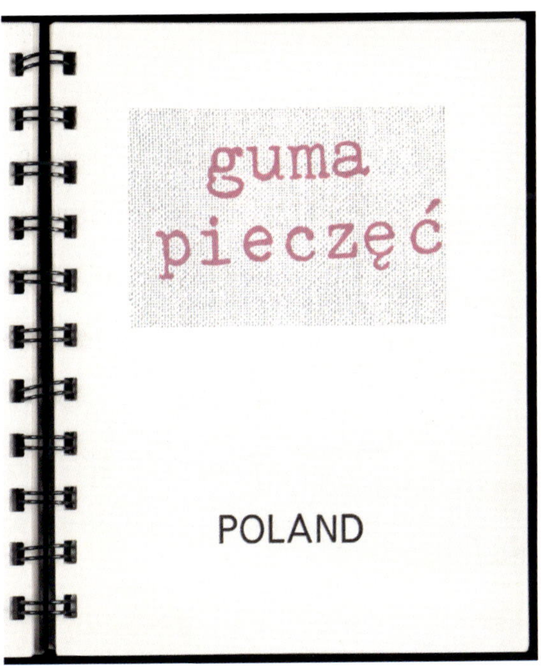
guma
pieczęć
POLAND

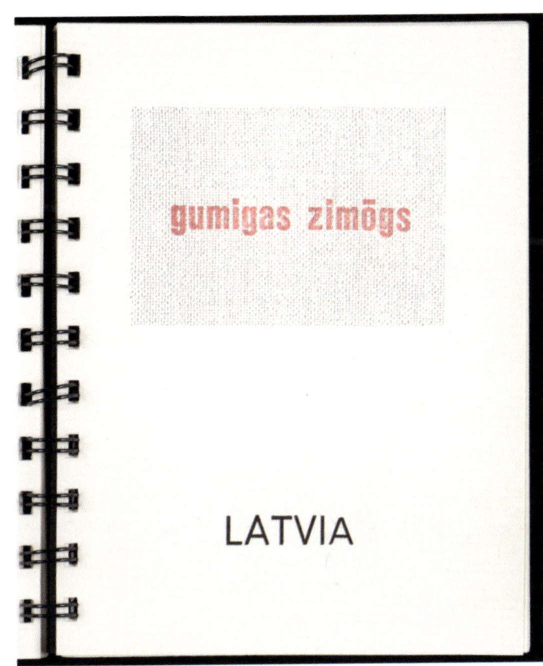
gumigas zimōgs
LATVIA

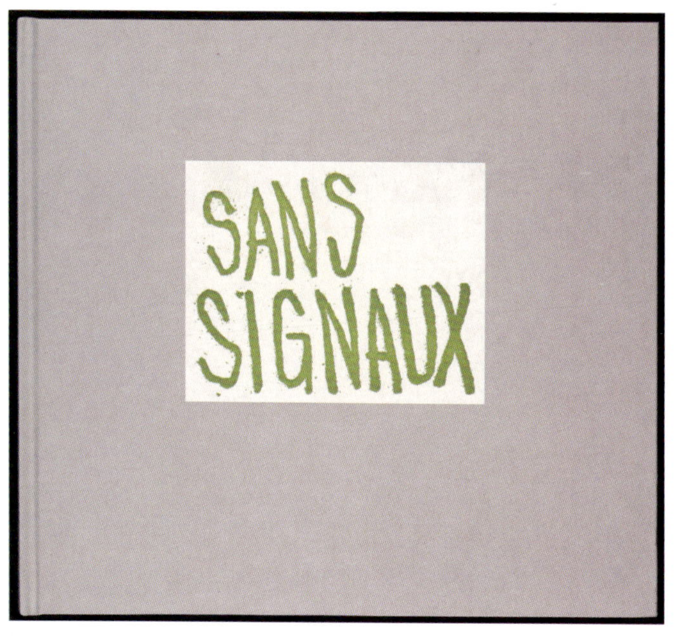


**Sans Signaux**

with Simon Cutts, Coracle, 1990

A collection of found signs whose title indicates, perhaps, that the collaborators took each from its original location, *Sans Signaux* is a kind of travel diary, recording quirky and unusual messages from shop windows in England, France, and Belgium. These very simple messages provide a clear sense of the character of the sign's maker and its setting. Removed from their usual contexts, these signs also highlight the inevitable idiosyncrasies found in words, phrases, and meanings that are specific to a particular place.

A related work *Stoppage, or, The Possibility of Mending Invisibly*, was published more than 15 years later using left-over materials from this edition.

## Short-Cuts

with Simon Cutts, Coracle, 2008

This title documents a collection of location-specific terms for "the names used in Britain for those narrow passageways between buildings, the short-cuts from street to street, the alleys which criss-cross between houses in a row." The format of *Short-Cuts*, an accordion-folded pamphlet, physically reflects the criss-crossing paths described by the text.

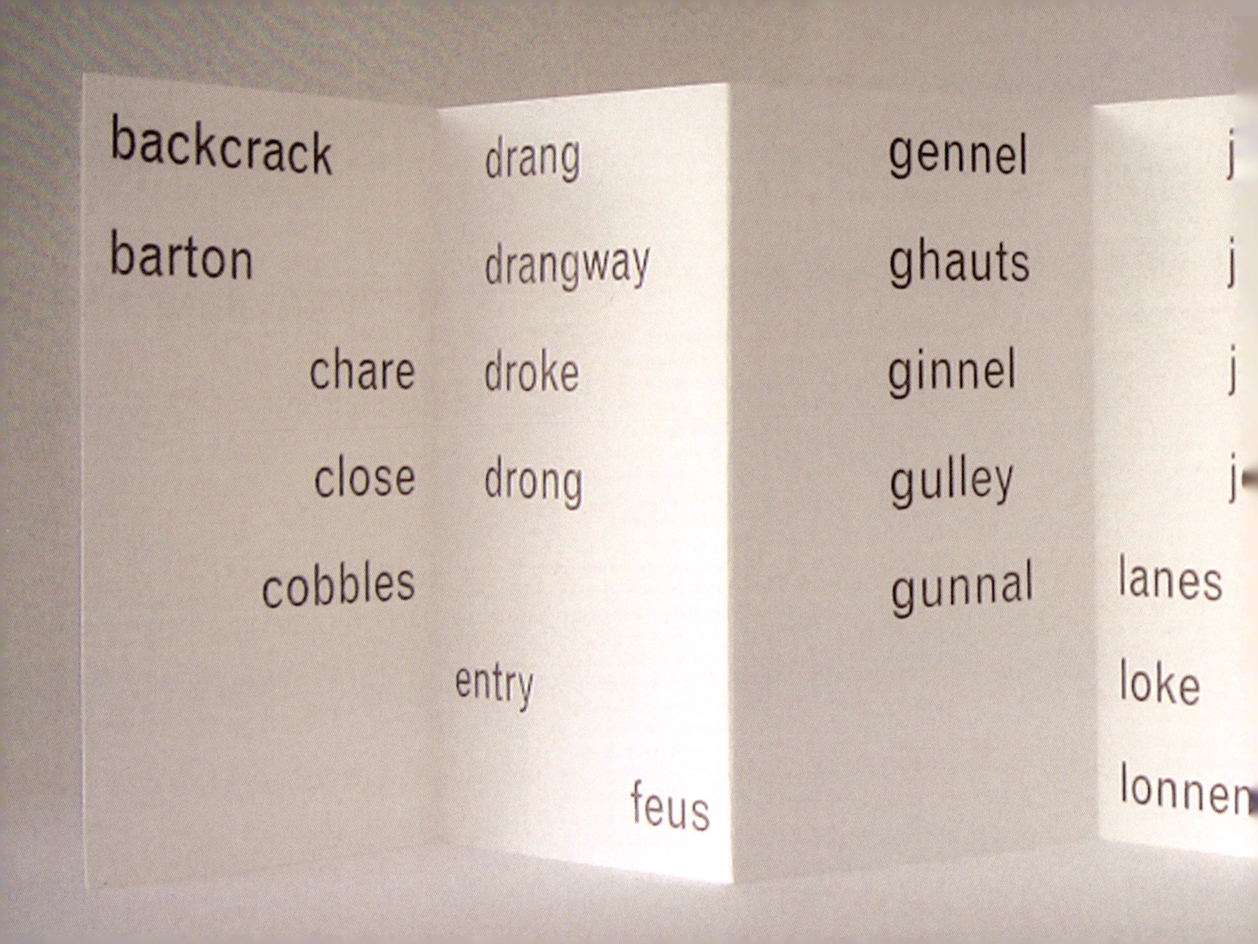

backcrack

barton

chare

close

cobbles

drang

drangway

droke

drong

entry

feus

gennel

ghauts

ginnel

gulley

gunnal

j

j

j

j

lanes

loke

lonnen

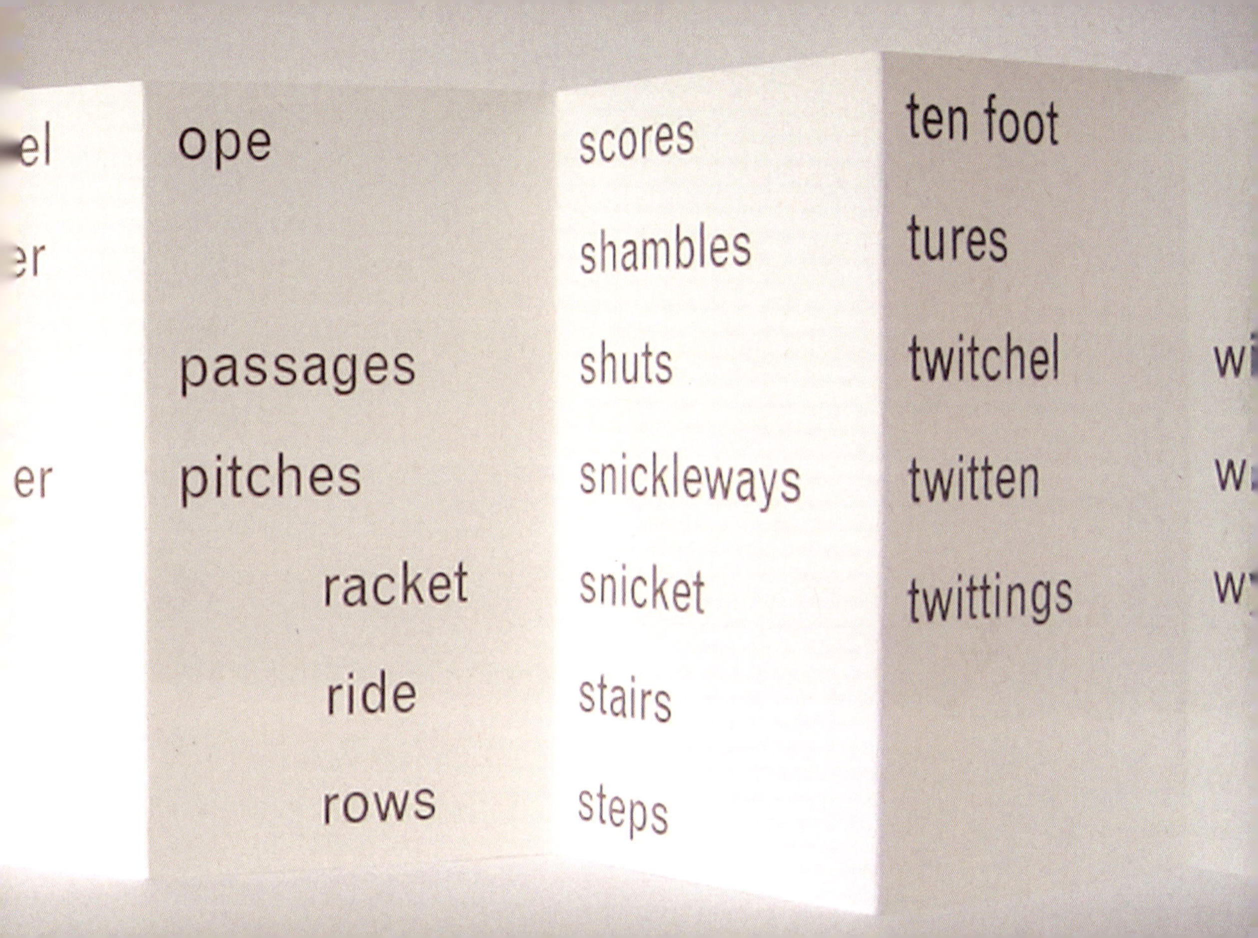
ope
passages
pitches
racket
ride
rows
scores
shambles
shuts
snickleways
snicket
stairs
steps
ten foot
tures
twitchel
twitten
twittings

# LEFT-OVERS

A distinctive feature of Erica Van Horn's work is the frequent recycling of materials left over from other projects or salvaged from daily life. "I have a long habit of not wasting anything" the artist writes, "[I have made] a great many books from the detritus of my own work process. For me, they retain all of the excitement and the imperative quality of the act of making." In addition to documenting her working process and the effort involved in bookmaking, Van Horn's practice of re-using saved and salvaged fragments reveals the ways such fragments make meaning. Histories and narratives can be embedded in ephemeral bits and pieces; scraps can carry substantial information. Re-worked and altered image and text fragments become visual representations of the incomplete and irregular nature of memory.

**Eighty-Nine Women Drawn in a Book:**
**10 February 1987–1 February 1988**
New York, 1988

Within a found financial ledger book (several pages of which contain figures and calculations) Van Horn blends drawing, painting, and collaged pages from magazines to create eighty-nine images of women. Re-using found materials in combination with her own drawing allows the artist to revise and re-imagine commercially produced depictions of women: a woman in a photographic advertisement, for instance, might be transformed into a portrait of Saint Lucy, who happens to be the patron saint of salesmen.

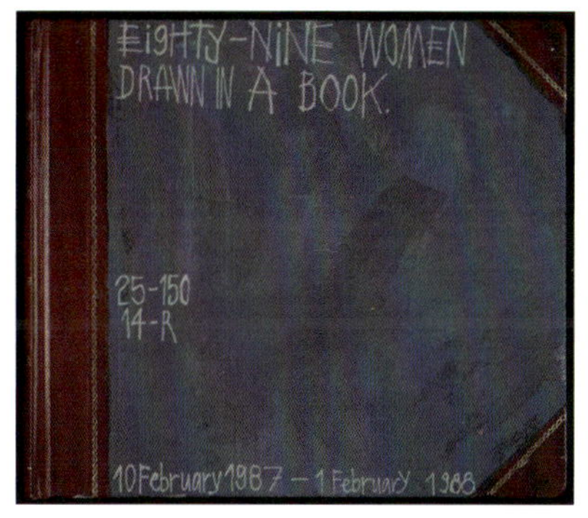


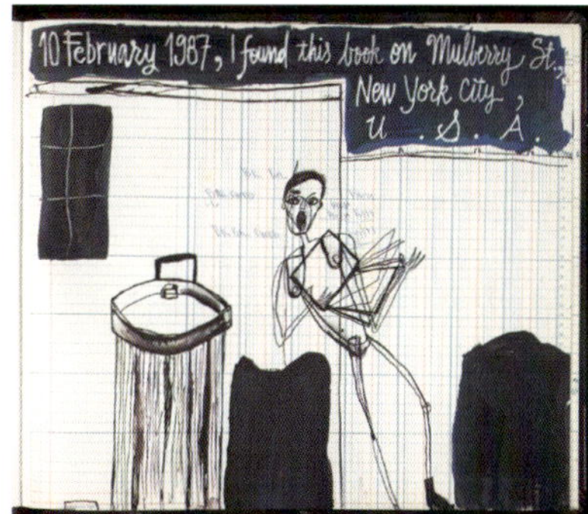

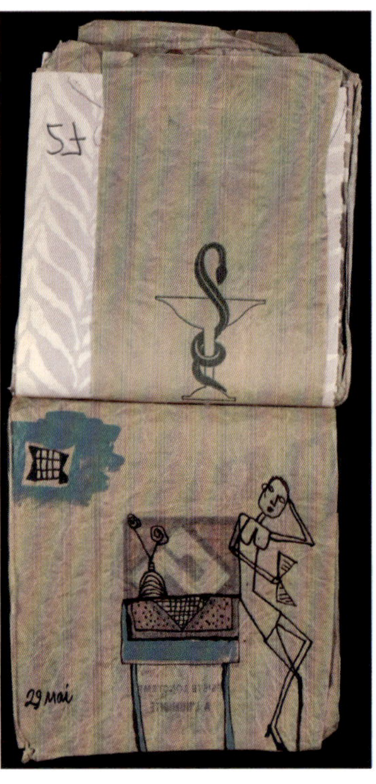


**On Fruit & Vegetable Bags, 31 Portraits, Self & Projected: One a Day, May 1986**

Paris, 1986

This book is the result of the daily practice, for 31 days, of making self-portraits. By drawing her own portrait—"self and projected"—each day, Van Horn documents the unglamorous daily work of the artist. Exploring her own image, day by day and into an as-yet-undescribed future, the book creates an unfolding visual autobiographical narrative, creating a record of the artist's evolving sense of herself. Of her choice of materials for this book, she writes "I loved the small paper bags given out in the greengrocers. This was a way to use them without having the bags be the focus. The bags were the everyday." *On Fruit & Vegetable Bags* reveals a complex of meanings in the reclamation, re-working, and re-use of the things of daily life, including the artist's self-image.

**Scraps of an Aborted Collaboration**

with Some One Else, Coracle, 1994

This short, image and text narrative relates the story of a failed collaborative project. Van Horn uses illustrations made for a proposed children's book, appearing here as details and incomplete pieces, alongside a distilled tale about her collaborator's failure to produce a promised text to accompany them. The book mimics the lined pages of a school notebook filled with handwritten text, establishing an atmosphere not unlike a children's book, creating a lively tension with the story's biting wit.

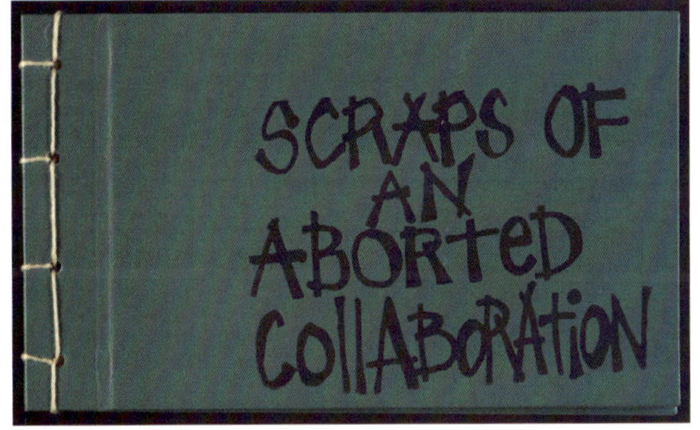

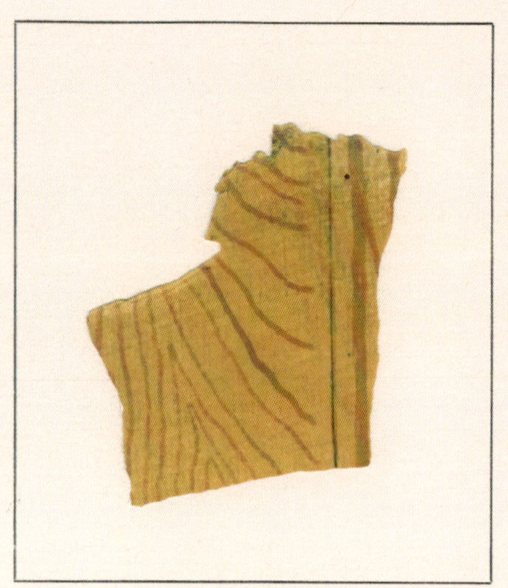

A PAINT-PEELING

from a table wood-grained by me in 1991
which peeled in the early winter of 1993.

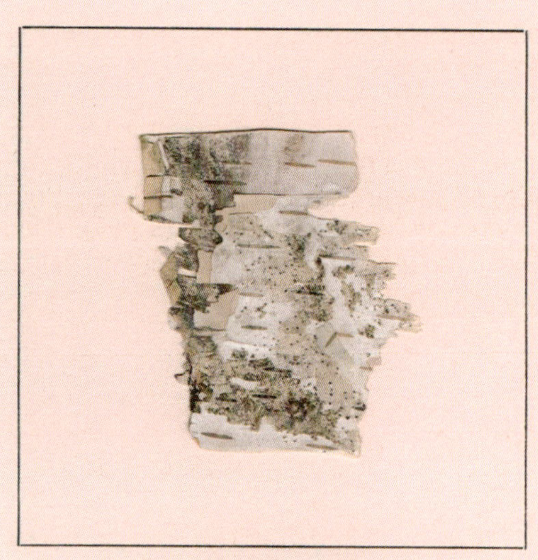

A BIRCH BARK PEELING

from a tree at Chestnut Pond, New Hampshire in 1988
layered in a drawer and forgotten until the spring of 2004
in Tipperary

**Two Peelings: 1993 & 2004**
Coracle, 2004

This modest pair of folded cards illustrates Van Horn's facility for locating complicated worlds of information in small remnants or fragments. In this case, the *Two Peelings* contain shadows of stories that cross time and space. The brief information on each card suggests absent narratives about the times of the initial interaction with these materials, when they were whole, and the artist's later re-discovery and presentation of them as incomplete peelings to be incorporated into new work. The brief text further locates the peelings by tying them to three primary homes—New Hampshire, where she grew up, and Docking, England, and Tipperary, Ireland, two places where she has lived for much of her adult life.

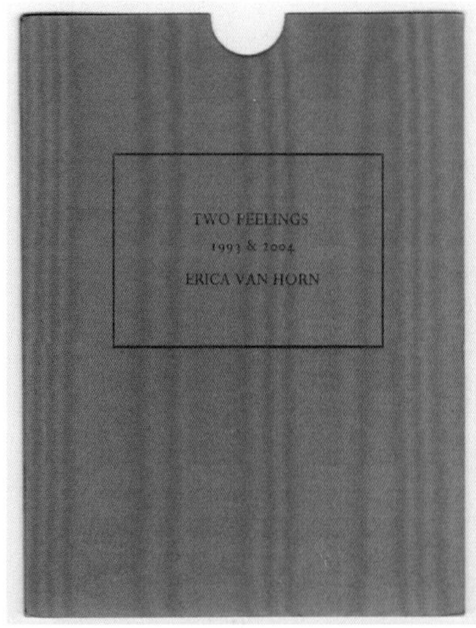

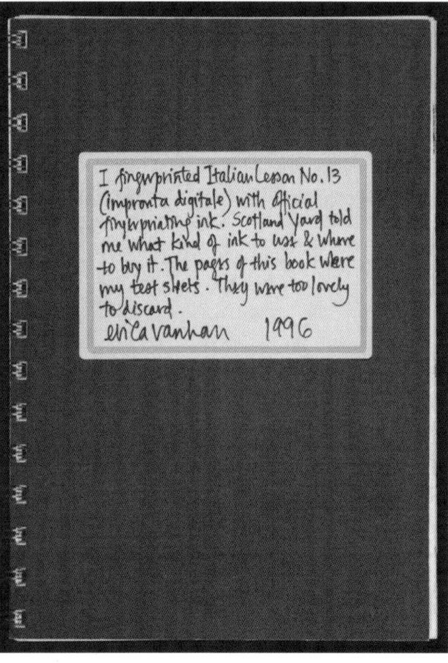


I Fingerprinted Italian Lesson no. 13 (Impronta Digitale) with Official Fingerprinting Ink: Scotland Yard Told Me What Kind of Ink to Use & Where to Buy It. The Pages of this Book were My Test Sheets. They Were Too Lovely to Discard.
London, 1996

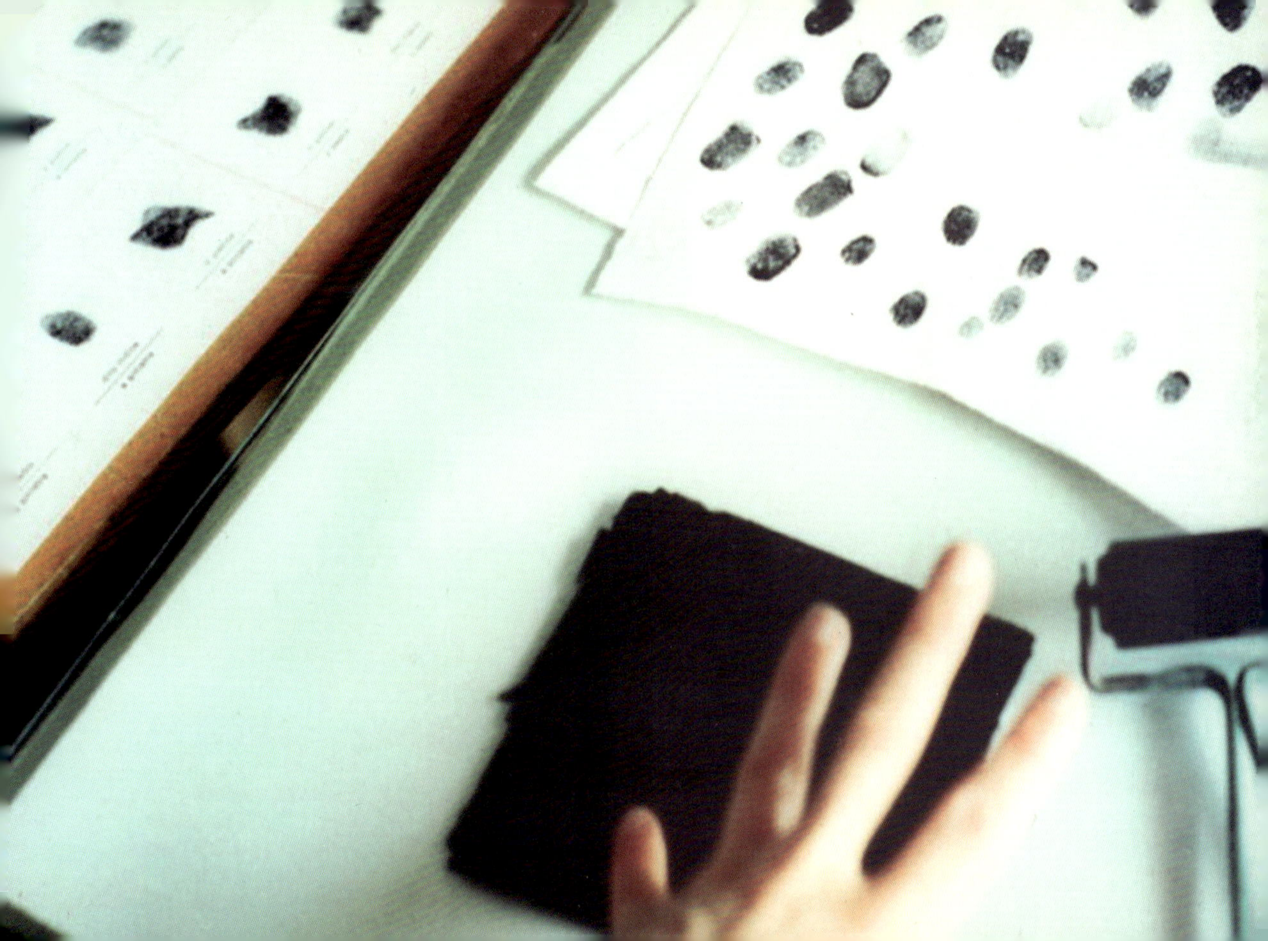

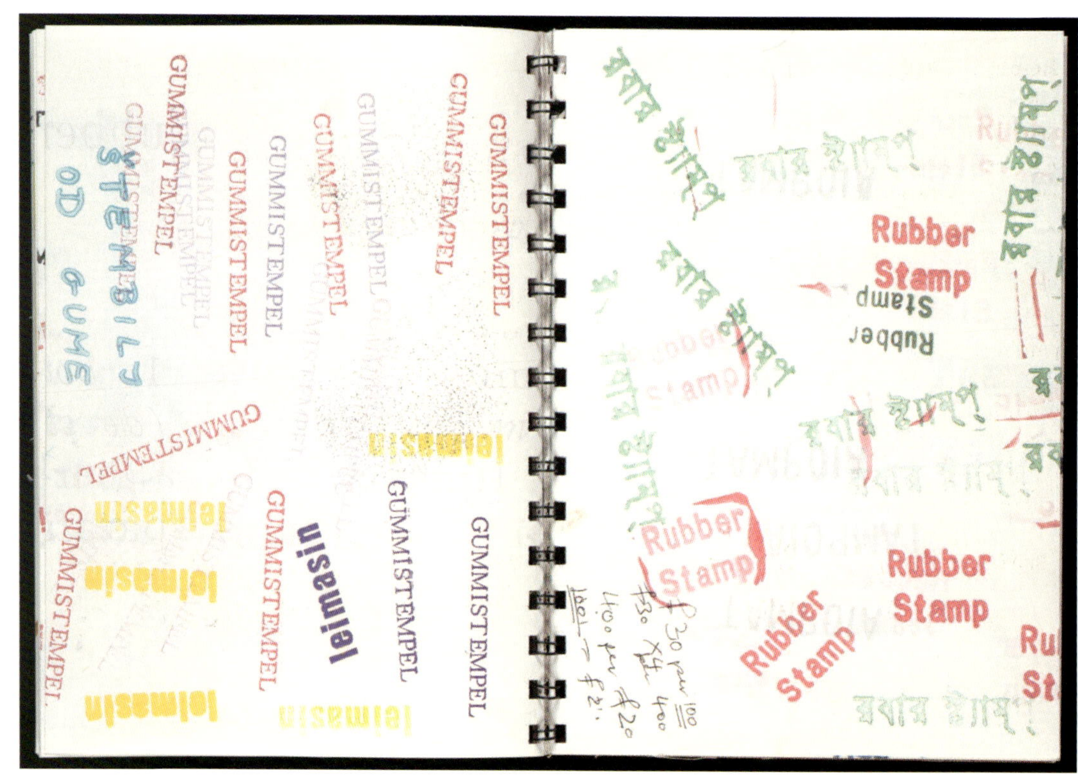
GUMMISTEMPEL
leimasin
Rubber Stamp
রবার স্ট্যাম্প

## A Remnant Book of Practice Pages for Gumigas Zimogs

London, 1996

This *Remnant Book* and *I Fingerprinted Italian Lessons No. 13* are examples of the practice of recycling the test sheets and trial pages created as by-products of making a book. "These books evolved from not wanting an integral part of the book-process to be lost" Van Horn writes. "After rubber stamping into 300 books, the practice pages stayed important as they reminded me of the point when the stamp colour and pressure was just right. The same was true for the perfecting of my own fingerprints." In addition to recording creative processes, these spin-off books are visually compelling in their own right, recognizing the appeal of visual pattern in unusual configurations and repetitions of print, color, and shape.

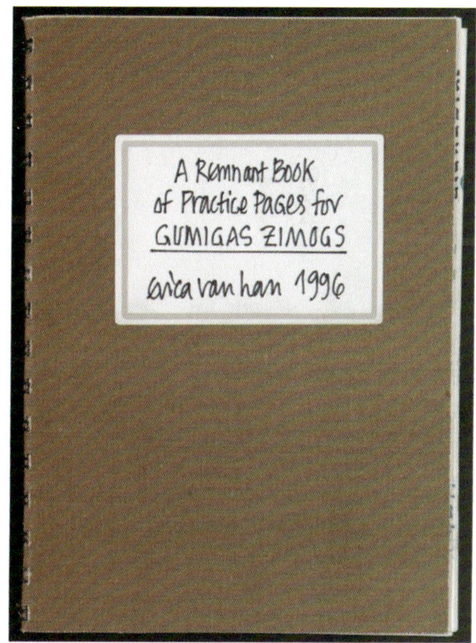

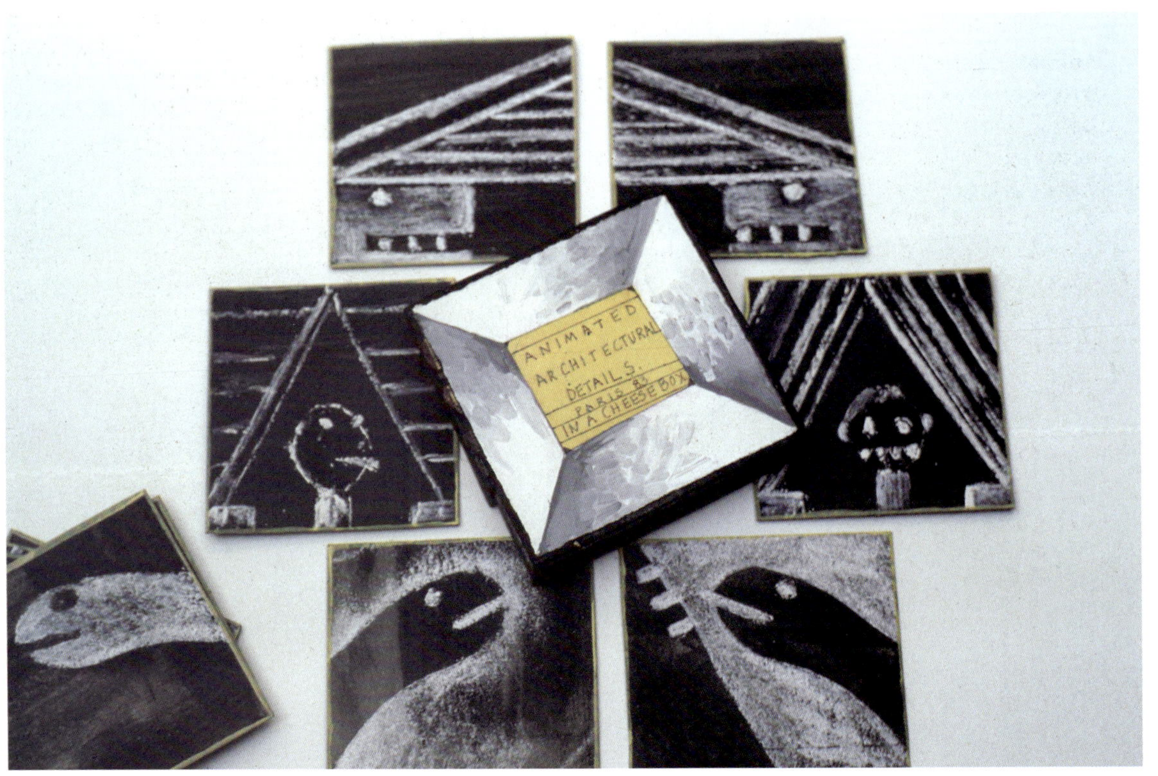
ANIMATED
ARCHITECTURAL
DETAILS.
PARIS 83
IN A CHEESE BOX

**Animated Architectural Details in a Cheesebox**

Paris, 1983

Living in France in the 1980s, Van Horn became interested in everyday materials which, though common to the specific community, seemed unusual and special. "I loved the little wooden cheeseboxes. I could never throw one away. They made lovely little containers for the small things I was observing. [In this case], the cheesebox became a kind of copybook for me… a way for me to gather together various gargoyles as isolated objects with the idea that their saved likenesses might be re-used in another form."

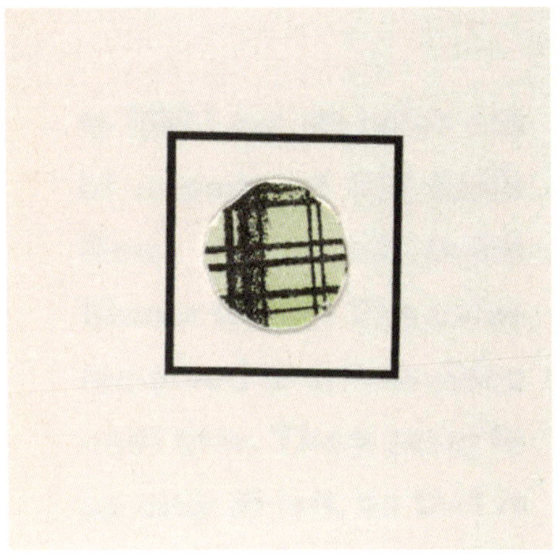

**Stoppage, or, The Possibility of Mending Invisibly**
Coracle, 2006

*Stoppage, or, The Possibility of Mending Invisibly* was published sixteen years after *Sans Signaux*, using leftover materials from that project: "In 1990 I cut 100 holes out of a page of the book *Sans Signaux* (with Simon Cutts). The holes remained in an envelope until now. There seem to be only 85 left, so that is the edition." The title of this piece refers back to the original project, but it can also be read as a reflection on Van Horn's process in making the work, the possibility or impossibility of making the artistic process invisible, and the aesthetic significance of mending or restoring something to usefulness.

**Some Words from that Letter**

Chicago, c.1985

The habit of re-using materials extends even to language in *Some Words from that Letter*. Produced in several variant editions, including this one in which several small concertinas are collected in a house-shaped box, this work uses text and image fragments to suggest a narrative: "*Some Words from that Letter* is the boxing-up of the end of a relationship. The letter signaled the end." The work acknowledges the letter as the central fact of the relationship's resolution, but by transforming its language into the raw materials of the books, the letter is cut loose from its original context. In this way, the letter is re-made, its content and possibilities re-imagined.

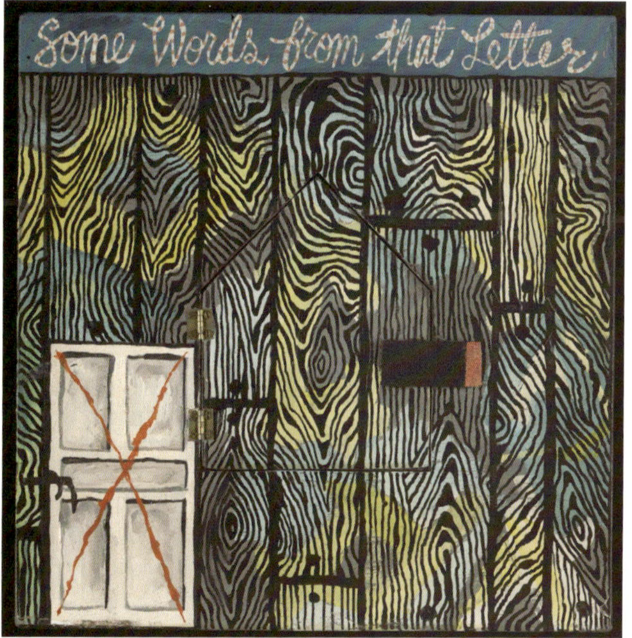

# WORLD OF INTERIORS

For more than fifteen years Erica Van Horn has collected, cataloged, and displayed paper envelope interiors, creating a large-scale, ongoing project that includes bookworks, collages and works on paper, public installations, and ephemera. "The only function of an envelope interior" she tells us, "is to hide the contents of the envelope." In focusing her interest on this most invisible example of visual pattern and image, the artist reveals the irony of her statement even as the envelope interior's function is transformed. *The World of Interiors* elevates a mundane and daily material to a more considered level; the value placed on both the simple visual patterns and the very paper on which they are printed calls attention to the role of beauty in a culture made up of disposable products. By exposing the interiors of printed envelopes and reassigning them to works of art and books, she upsets our expectations about her seemingly ordinary materials.

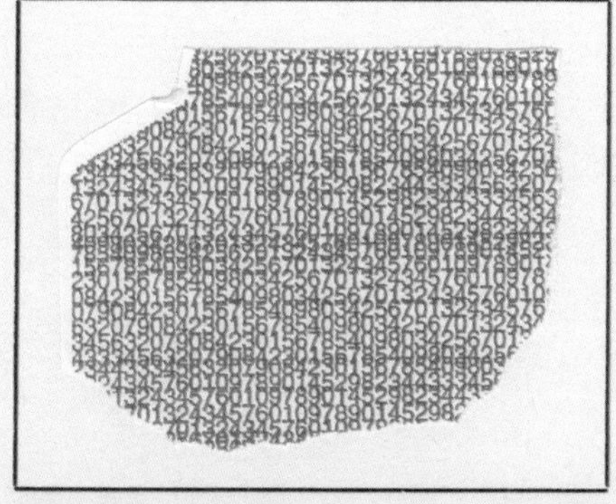

ENVELOPE
INTERIOR
NUMBER 456

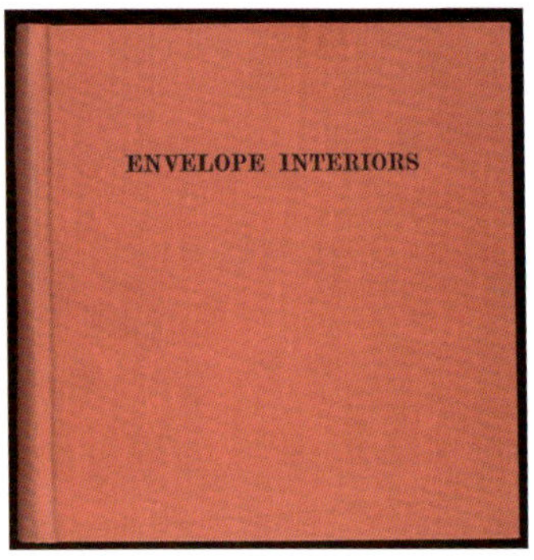


The idea for this collection of envelope interiors is not my own. It came from David Bellingham, and I believe he was composing his own book to document his own bits of his own envelopes. I hope he will forgive my appropriation of the project, as I felt that such a scrapbook belonged as much in the world of train spotting or stamp collecting as in the world of art.

This is one of 9 books, which may take me a while to finish because I will be filling the spaces as I find the envelopes. I will stay inside the lines.

Erica Van Horn
Begun 23 SEP 1995
Finished 09 FEB 1996

## Envelope Interiors

Coracle, 1996

Describing the inspiration for this book (the idea of collecting envelope interiors was borrowed from her friend, artist David Bellingham), Erica Van Horn writes, "I felt that such a scrapbook belonged as much in the world of train spotting or stamp collecting as in the world of art." By extension, this volume suggests that collecting can be an art form, one that values daily practice, a careful eye, a completist sensibility. Attending to the acts of gathering and sorting her materials, she makes an art of the activities of collecting and organizing the envelope interiors used in her work. *Envelope Interiors* was made in an edition of only nine copies, each hand assembled over time as she acquired the requisite number of envelope interiors. Describing the edition, she wrote, "nine books… may take me a while to finish because I will be filling the spaces as I find the envelopes. I will stay inside the lines."

## Boy Bell's Book of Envelope Interiors

Coracle, 1994

As an artist who often collaborates with other artists, writers, and printers, in *Boy Bell's Book of Envelope Interiors* she acknowledges the increasingly public nature of her envelope interior works: "many people have now been alerted to the exciting world of envelope interiors. Friends have allowed me to rifle through their rubbish, or to sit nearby when they open their mail. Without being asked, people started collecting for me." This volume lists the locations of some sources, which include Ireland, England, and the United States.

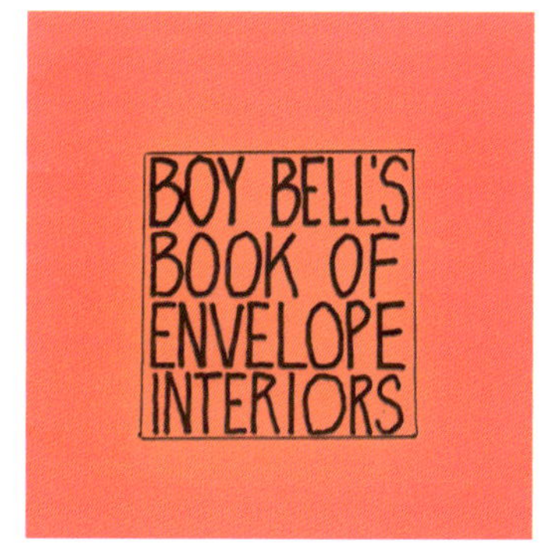


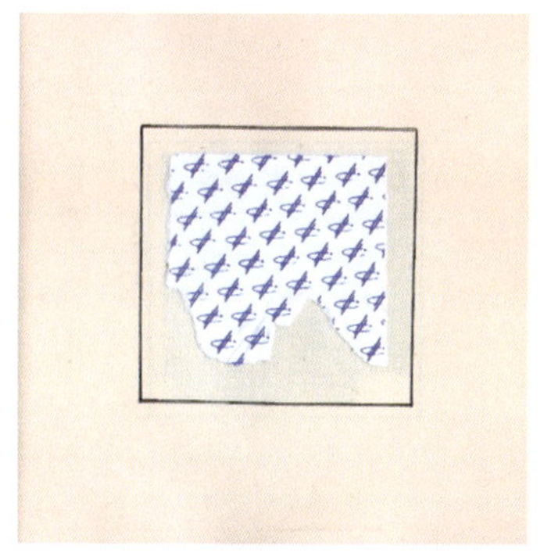

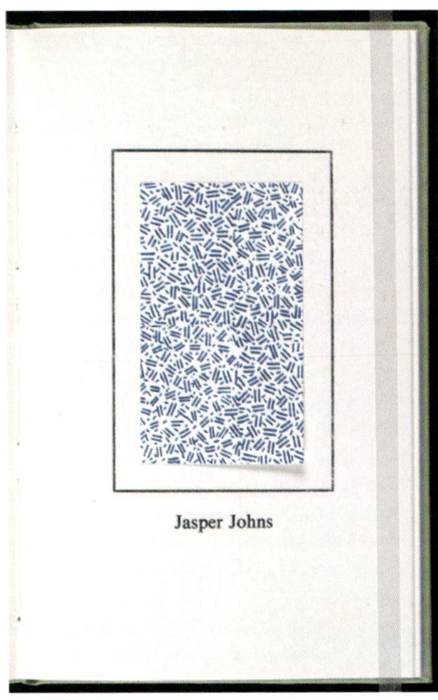
Jasper Johns

**Envelope Interior Art History**

with Harry Gilonis, Coracle, 1997

In this witty envelope interior album, Van Horn and her collaborator Harry Gilonis see the work of various important artists in a collection of repeated visual patterns. The collaborators assign envelope interior patterns to artists whose work they would or could typify: a repeating sequence of green leaves is attributed to environmental artist Andy Goldsworthy; a map-like image is credited to Richard Long, an artist who includes maps and landscape elements in his work; a consistent pattern of lines represents the work of abstract artist Agnes Martin. The featured artists include modern and conceptual artists, such as Jasper Johns and Sol LeWitt, alongside more classical artists, such as Gustave Caillebotte, whose famous painting *Paris Street, Rainy Day* (1877) is represented by a pattern depicting two figures walking under an umbrella.

### Envelope Interior Pin-Up Calendar

Coracle, 1997–1999

This series of hand-assembled calendars, each using twelve unique interior papers, present a kind of self-referential turn in the envelope interiors projects. As a whole the project celebrates commonplace materials and employs them to make art objects; using these materials to accompany letterpress-printed calendars highlights the everyday quality of the papers and the value of art in our daily lives. The calendars also comment on and revise the idea of more traditional 'pin up' calendars, featuring photographs of women: "I thought to use the same term but to display something that I thought was interesting and at least as varied as women's bodies. My pin-ups were labour intensive—lots of letterpress printing and pasting in the interiors obsessively one at a time. Every 12-month grouping was different, while the world of naked lady pin-ups is all about shiny paper and airbrushing and achieving a safe sameness to the commodity being displayed."

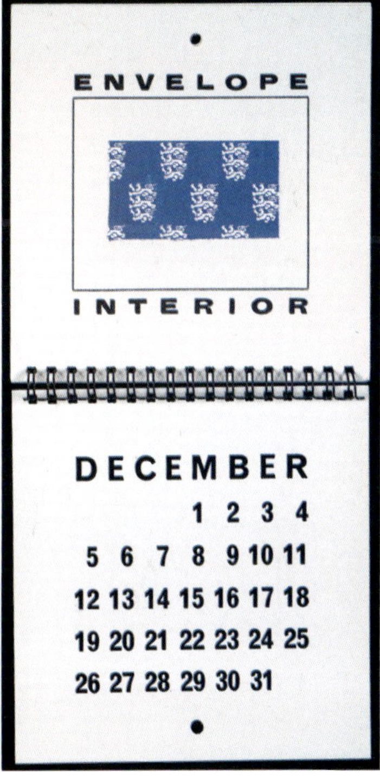

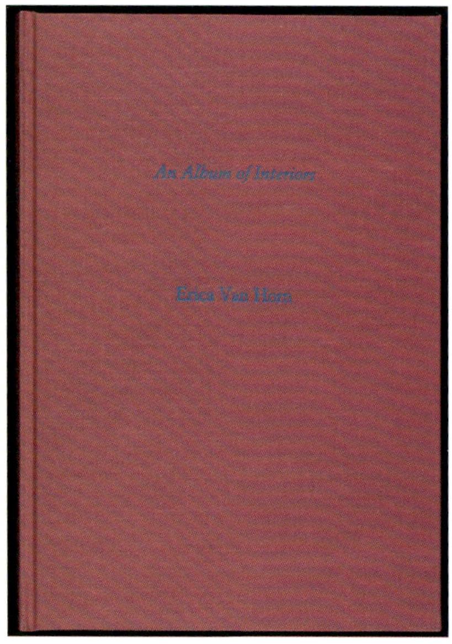


## Album of Interiors

Coracle, 2008

As what the artist calls "emblems of materiality and tactility in an increasingly electronic world of information," she finds, "the continued use of content-obscuring interior envelope patterns a cause of much surprise and wonder." This album includes fourteen samples along with descriptions of the ways each either exemplifies some feature of the broader World of Interiors or represents an anomaly or significant variance from the norm. The personal nature of the project of collection and exhibition of envelope interiors is revealed in the artist's poignant private associations to the paper samples.

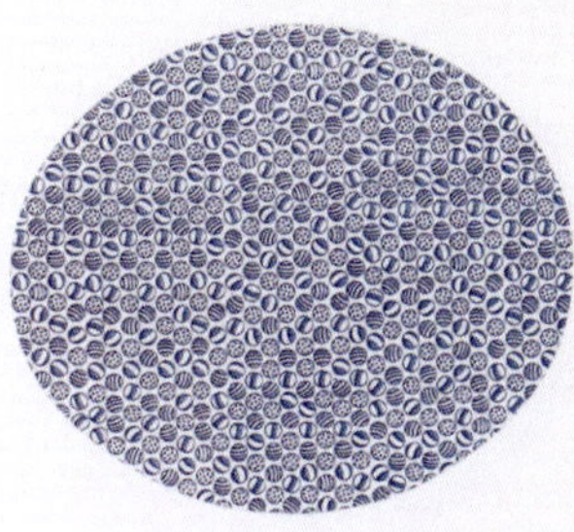

My friend Tullio loved this envelope interior. No matter how many new and exciting ones I discovered, this remained his favorite. When he became very ill with cancer, we discussed the idea of me doing a wall of interiors for him in his flat. He spent a long time deciding which wall should be done. We discussed how often this particular interior would be used in relation to all of the other interiors. We discussed light and the possible problem of fading. Then I got busy with other projects, and his illness progressed. We never even got the wall started before he died. Everything happened faster than we could have imagined. It is ten years later and I never look at this envelope interior without thinking of him.

Most envelope interiors are printed in blue. A fair number are black or grey. After those come green ones which are often announcing their recycled status. Red is rare and yellow even more rare. I have no idea why something which the Royal Mail calls Electronic Services even needs an envelope.

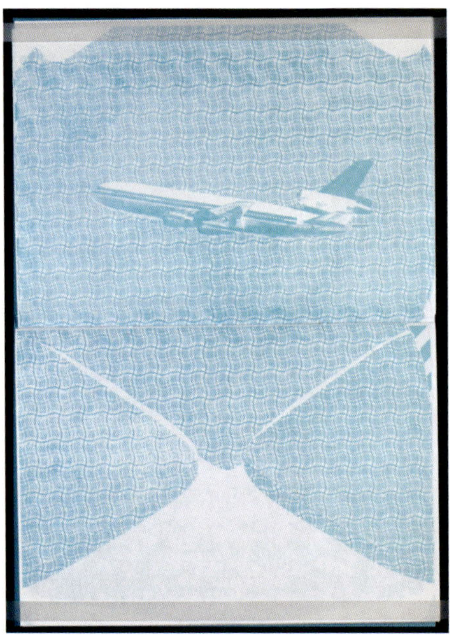

**Airmail Envelope Interiors**

with Simon Cutts, Coracle, 2002

A specific variation on the theme, this book features samples of airmail envelopes, emphasizing the peculiarities of their variance from other interiors; made of very thin and lightweight paper, their translucence allows text incorporated into the interior patterns to be read from the exterior of the envelope. Likewise, some are so thin that the handwritten addresses on their exteriors bleed through to the now-exposed interiors. As airmail envelopes become less common, this simple album also documents the passing away of a once-ubiquitous piece of material culture.

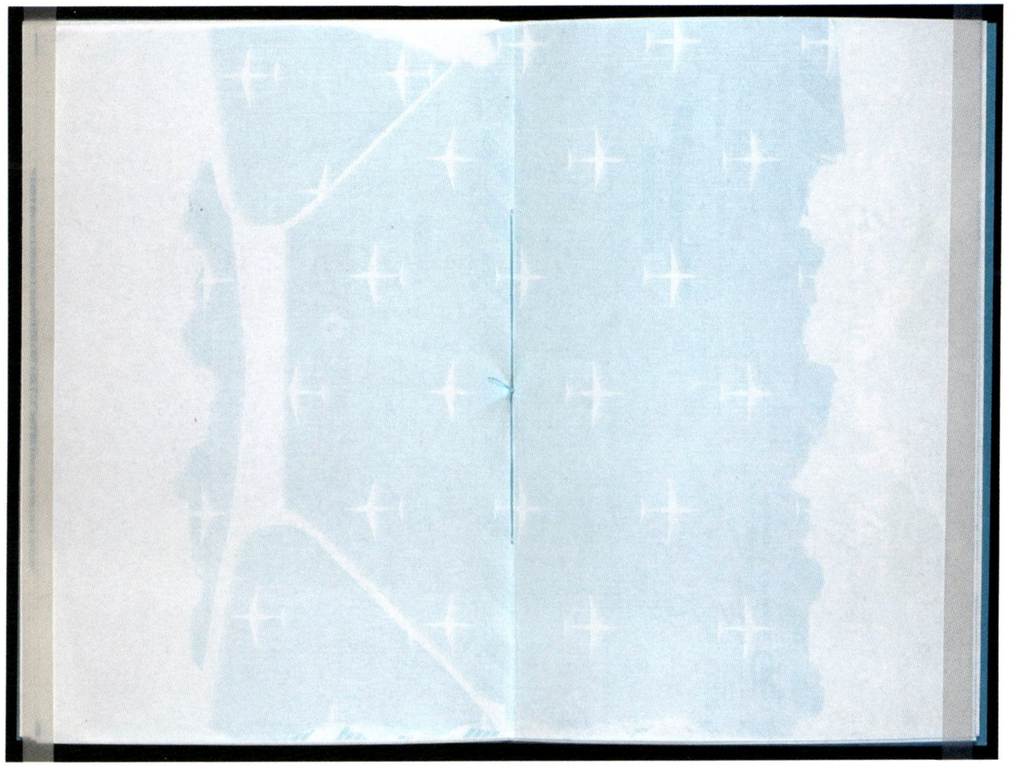

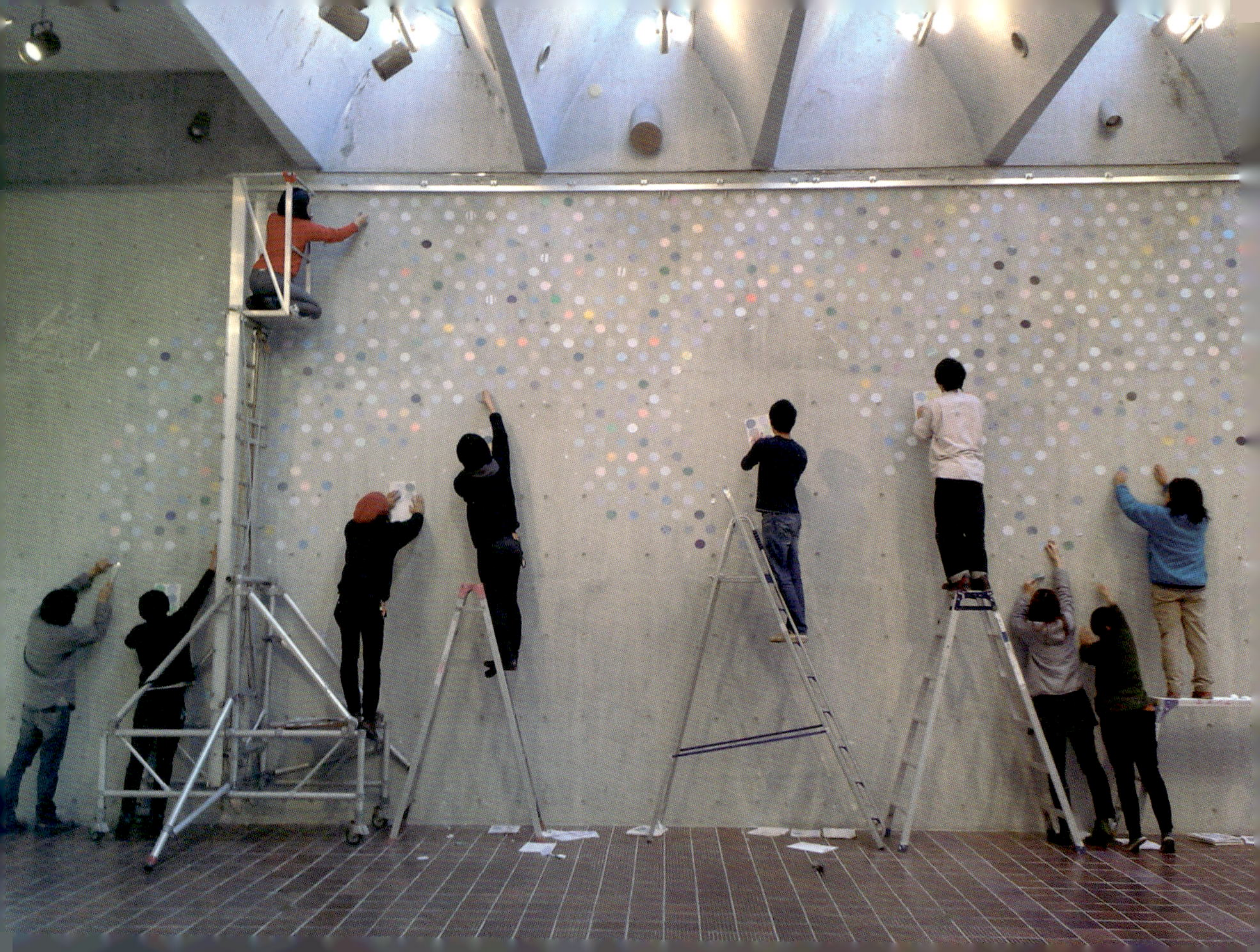

## De-installing The World of Interiors

Aichi University Museum, Japan, November 2008

In addition to book works and collages, Van Horn has created numerous public installations of envelope interiors. Without losing site of her material's original purpose—"[to] attempt to hide what [is] within: the money, the figures, the message"—her physical installations cut open, reveal, and display these otherwise hidden patterns in public space, complicating their meaning and generating new associations to this familiar material.

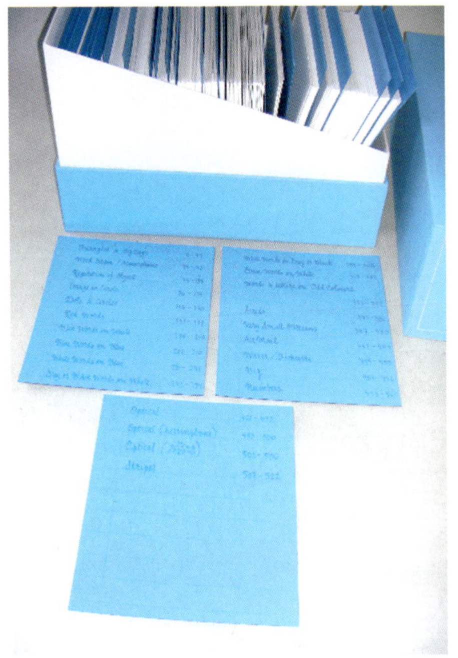

**Envelope Interior Reference File**

Ireland, 2007

After more than a decade of collecting and making art with the patterned interiors of commercially printed envelopes, Erica Van Horn created the *Envelope Interior Reference File*, a carefully organized index of her collection, including more than 500 letterpress printed file cards, each bearing a sample of envelope interior paper. The cards are arranged by category, including headings such as 'Red Words', 'Very Small Patterns', 'Airmail', 'Triangles', and 'Big', each of which is written on various section markers, allowing the artist's own handwriting to become part of the pattern-scape of the file. Of creating the *Reference File*, Van Horn writes: "The building of the file index box announces the end of trying to keep track of the seemingly endless envelope interior variations. Finding the descriptive headings to categorize various forms of zig-zags, and subtle differences has made me a bit crazy... The box is covered with a blue buckram to approximate the colour most often used in the actual interiors."

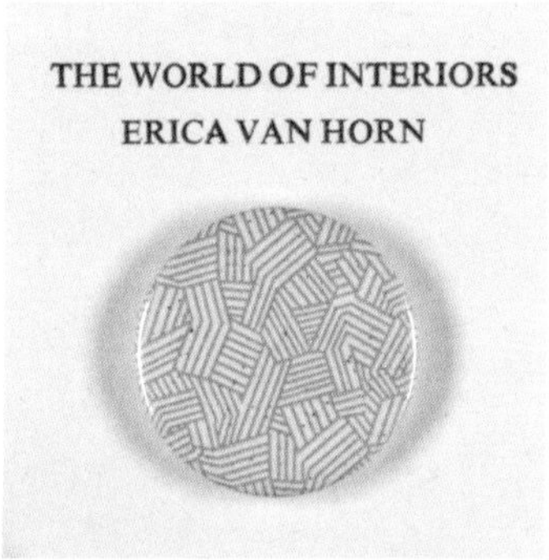

THE WORLD OF INTERIORS
ERICA VAN HORN

# NARRATIVE AND PATTERN

In her books, Erica Van Horn often explores the elements of visual narrative and the ways those elements might be exploited and subverted within the linear structure of the book. In an entirely modern reinterpretation of the heavy use of patterns found in the borders and backgrounds of much Medieval art, the recurrence of visual patterns frame and shape scenes and figures, underscoring what might be thought of as plot in visual narratives. Graphics suggest lively, dramatic, and compelling stories with little or no text and everyday patterns like the number and grid pattern of the calendar, or the irregular loops and swirls of cursive handwriting are infused with narrative significance. Van Horn's frequent use of the accordion format, which looks and functions like a book but can also be unfolded to reveal a many-paneled panorama, provides her narratives with a page-by-page pace while also calling to mind the scope and grandeur of panoramic images. In the tradition of 19th-century panoramic paintings she uses the form to depict landscapes, narrative scenes, or combinations of the two; in this way, these works can be viewed as idiosyncratic visual maps or illustrated memoirs.

**Odyssey**

Paris, 1982

*Odyssey* documents Van Horn's first trip to Paris; recording the artist's steps through the city, the book is both a personal map and an illustrated daily journal. The accordion format highlights the continual unfolding of the story. About the heavy use of patterning in this book, she writes "My first trip to Paris was a mission to explore and spend time with Medieval art. I wanted to learn about another way of making pictures. I had not expected to be so excited by the city itself. I tried to apply the world I was studying to the world in which I was living."

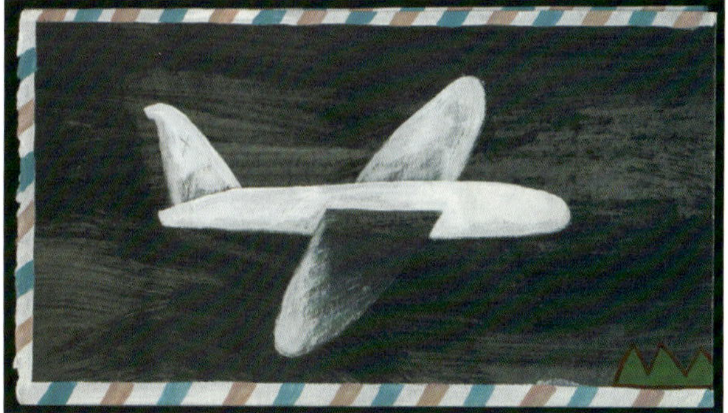

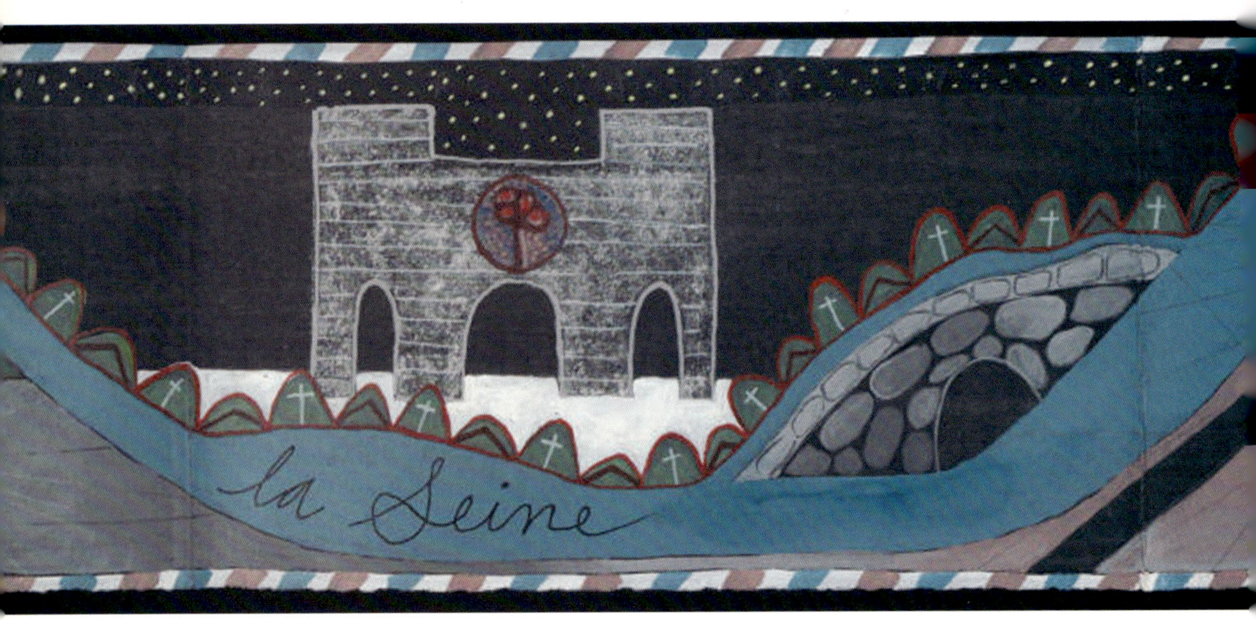
la Seine

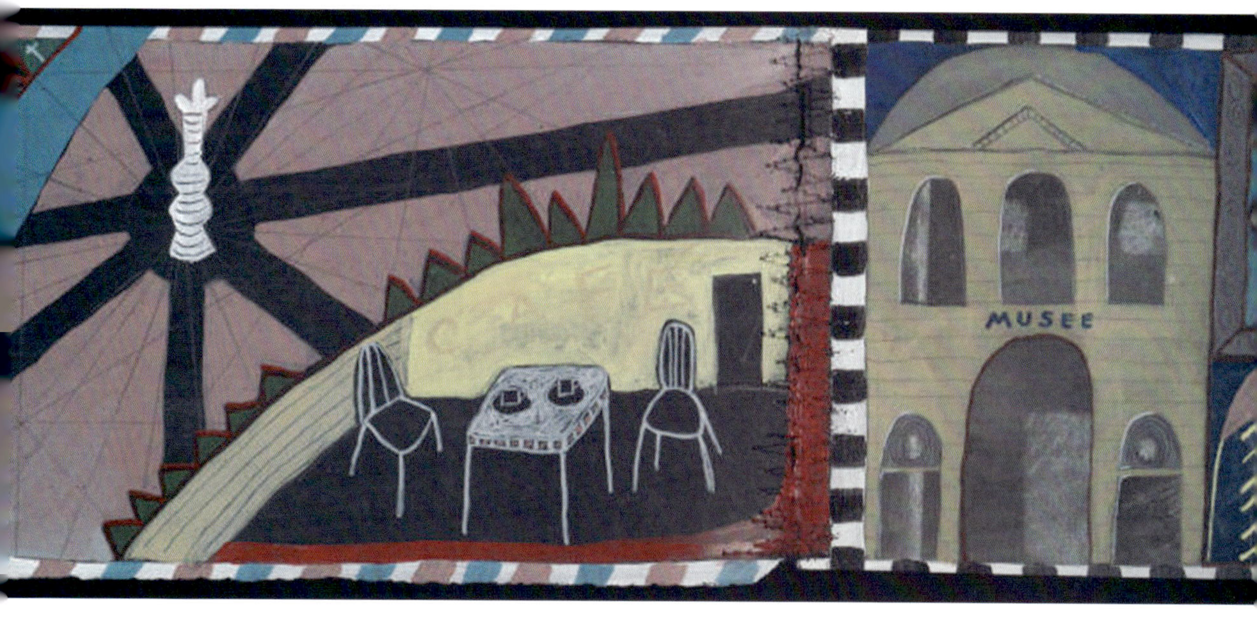
MUSEE

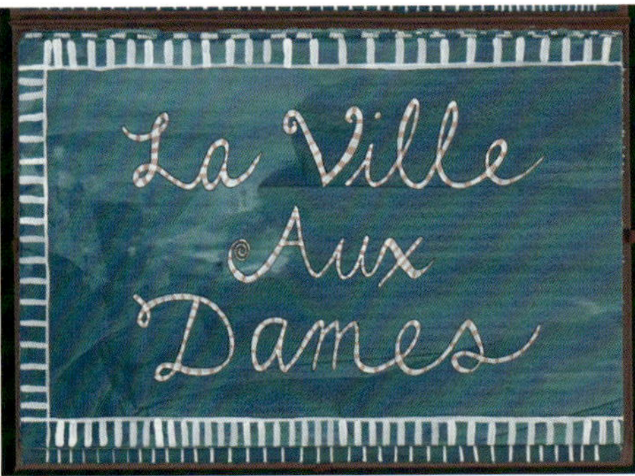


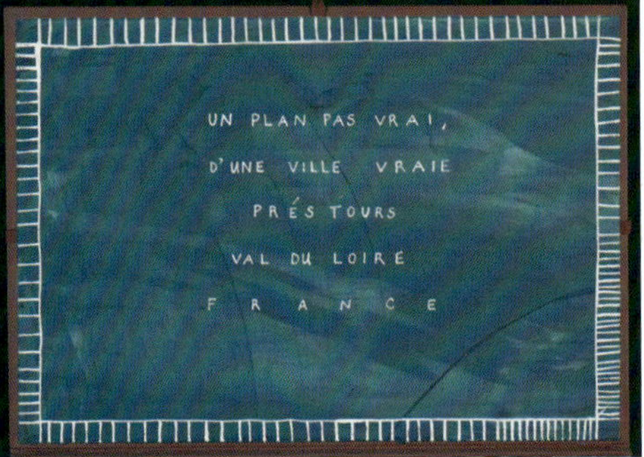


**La Ville Aux Dames**

Paris, 1983

*La Ville Aux Dames* is the "fictional plan for a real city: La Ville aux Dames is an actual town in the Loire, not far from Tours. When I first visited, I anticipated beautiful streets all named after famous women in French history. Instead, I found an antiseptic new town, with very little beauty to celebrate these women." In this enormous accordion book, the City of Women is re-imagined to include elegant boulevards surrounded by visual patterns incorporating female forms and abstract representations of buildings and other features of the town.

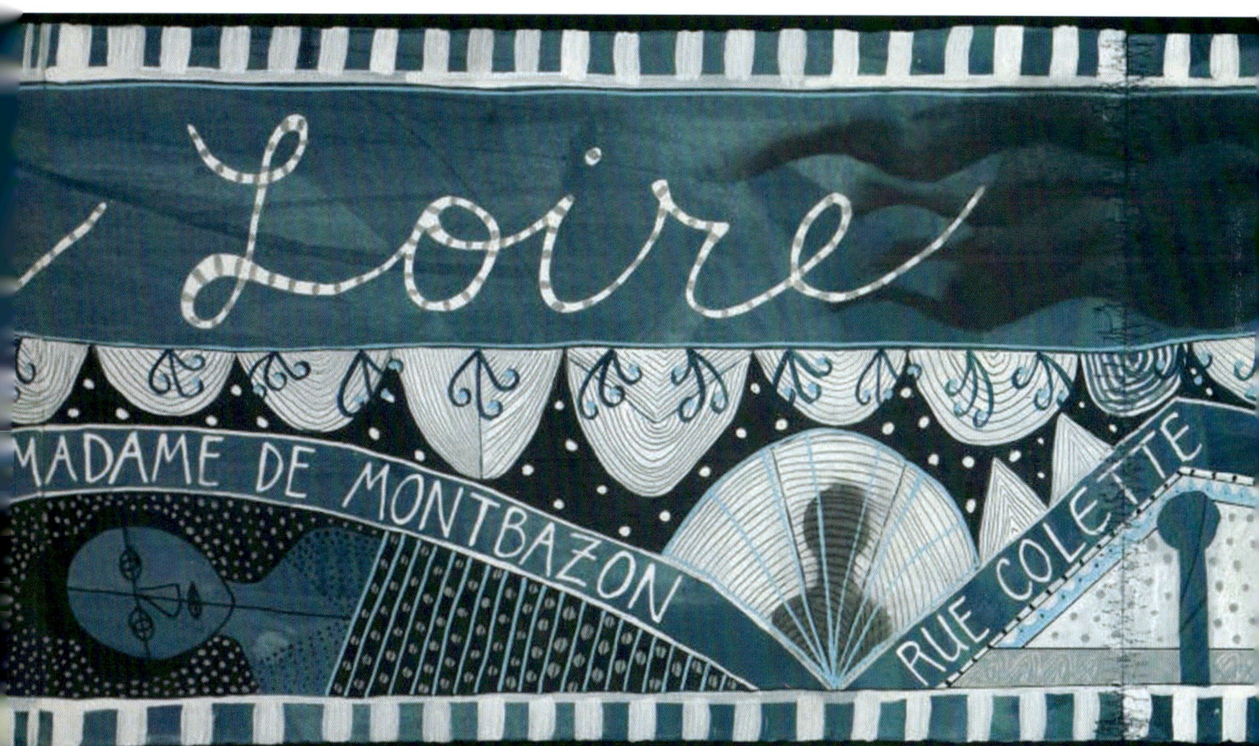
Loire
MADAME DE MONTBAZON
RUE COLETTE

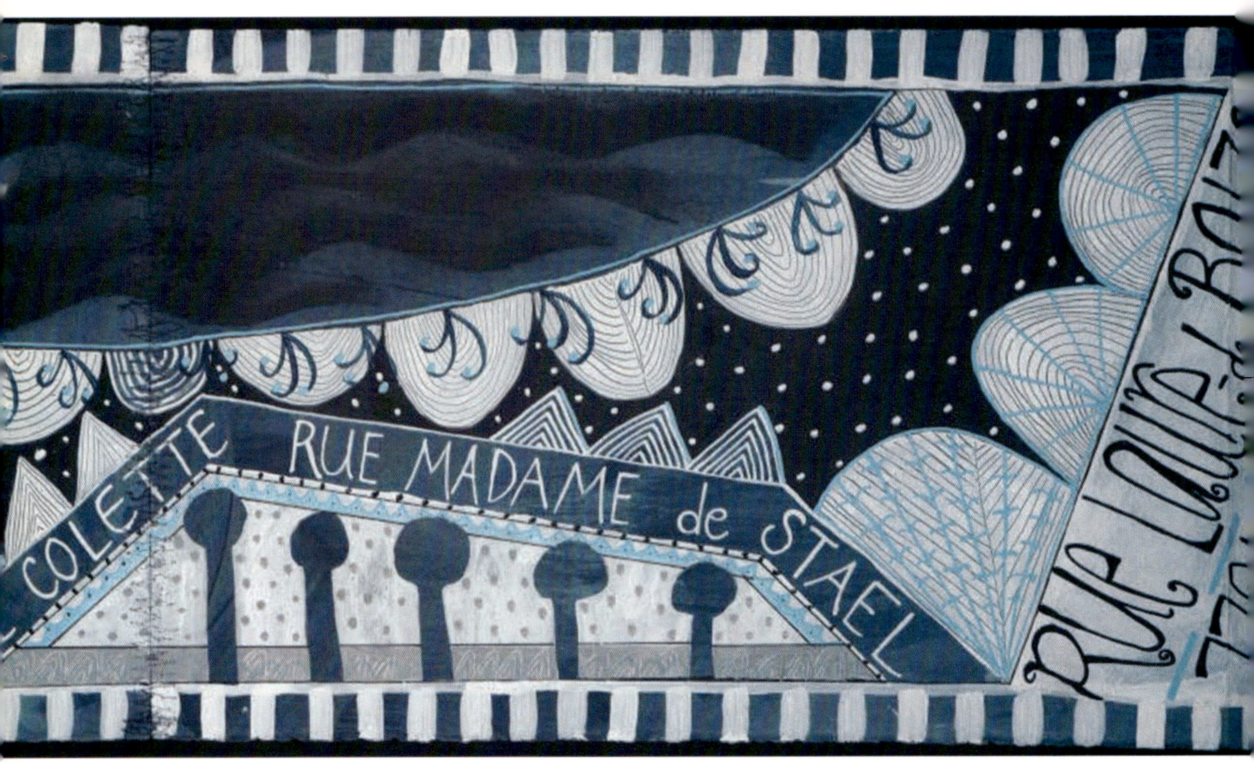
COLETTE
RUE MADAME de STAEL

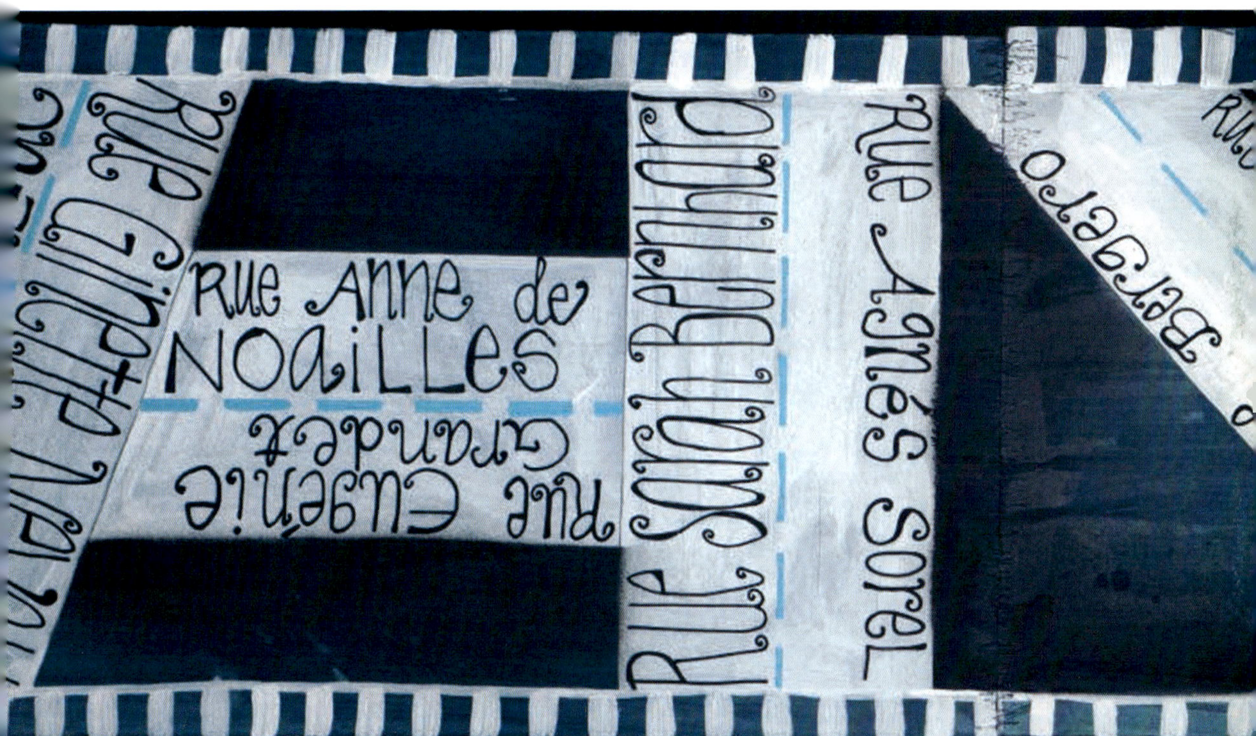

Rue Anne de
NOAILLES
Rue Eugénie
Grandet
Rue Agnès Sorel

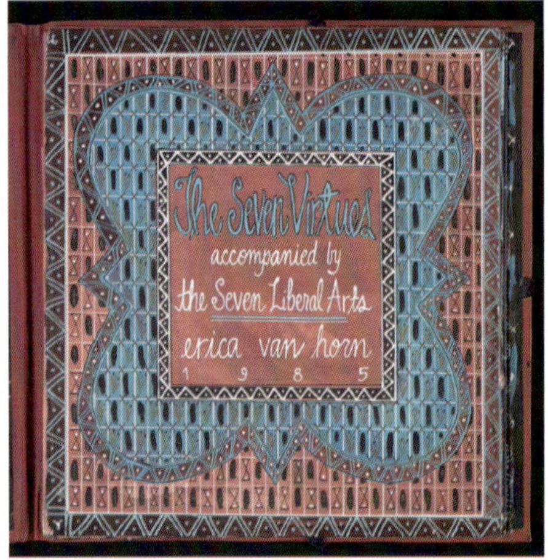


### The Seven Virtues
### (Accompanied by the Seven Liberal Arts)

Paris, 1985

Inspired in part by medieval art, *The Seven Virtues* reveals an abiding interest in manipulating pattern. Describing this large accordion format book, Van Horn writes: "*The Seven Virtues* is mostly an excuse for me to continue the obsessive patterning and storytelling which I love from medieval art. Combining the structure with a looser drawing style makes that world mine, not a fake relic." The influence of medieval art is present in the artist's work throughout the 1980s, though its elements are transformed and thoroughly modernized through her interpretation.

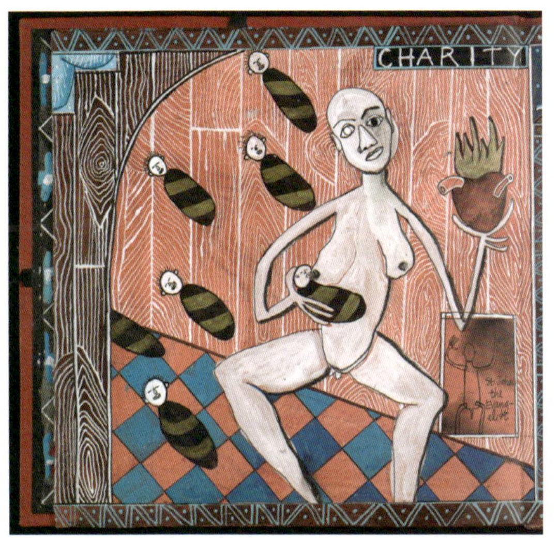
CHARITY

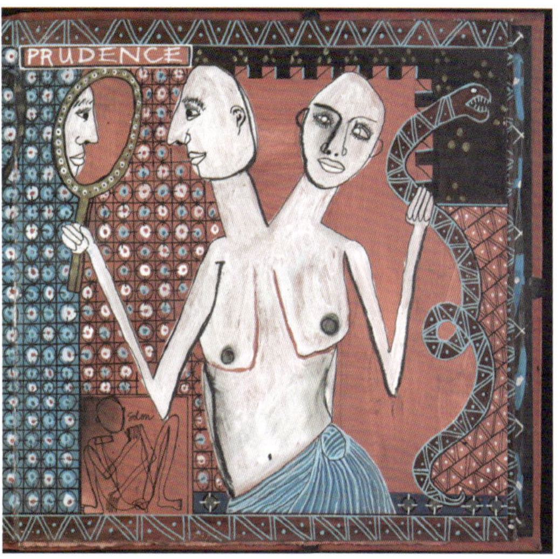
PRUDENCE

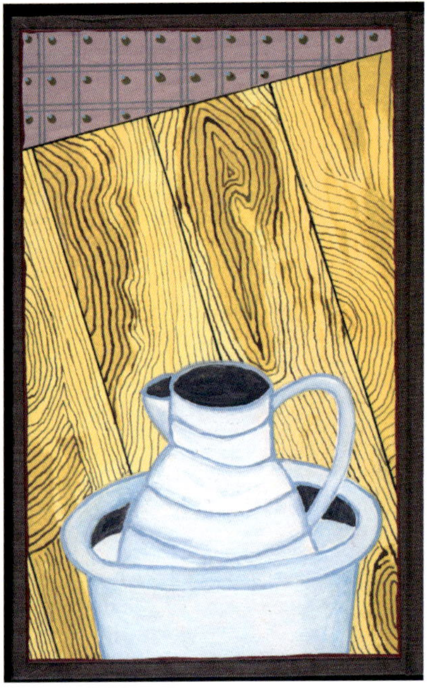

**Yellow Wood-Grained Table**

Paris, 1986

The very exaggerated wood-grained surface of the table in this work makes the surface as significant as the objects it holds, creating a curious still life in which the focal point of the painting seems to shift foreground to background and back. Remarking on the format, Van Horn calls this work "a folding painting, a kind of non-religious version of a retable." The accordion structure makes this a text-less book, a visual sequence of tabletop images unfolding panel by panel.

**Illuminated Books #18: Demon Tumbling Down Stairs**
Paris, 1988

These painted books are "a bit of play with the term Illuminated Book." This spine-painting is, also, an inversion of the rare and beautiful book art of fore-edge painting, in which landscapes and narrative scenes are painted on the edges of a splayed open book's pages. The artist struck upon this unusual format "as a way for people who have no wall space to have a painting, and for people who don't read to have books." To make her *Illuminated Books*, Van Horn purchased inexpensive books at a used bookstore in Paris, until the bookseller discovered what she was doing with them—wiring them together and rendering them unreadable—and refused to sell her any more.

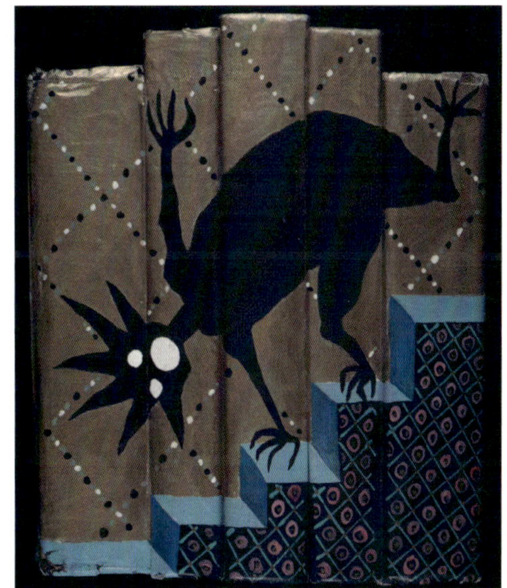

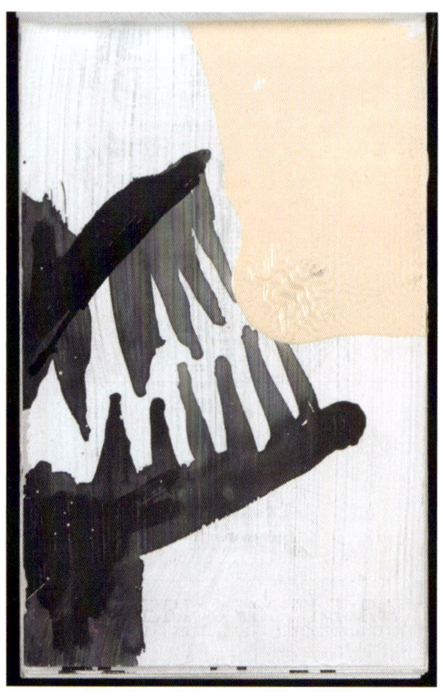

**Black Dog White Bark**
New York, 1986

This unique hand-painted book was later produced in a printed edition, which described the work as a collaboration: "text by Louis Asekoff, drawings by Erica Van Horn." The work "evolved from a conversation with the poet Louis Asekoff. What I refer to as his story was nothing more than the four words which stayed with me after the talking." *Black Dog White Bark* experiments with the barest elements of narrative. This hand-painted edition is made up of cards advertising an earlier exhibition, recycled for use as painted pages.

**Un Oeuf et Une Chaise**
Vitry-sur-Seine, 1983

In this imagistic autobiography, the artist records an "awkward time… thinking I was pregnant while very poor and living alone in Paris and not having a clue as to what I would do about it." The narrative is concentrated in its most basic elements: "I reduced the problem to two elements: the egg and the chair, literally waiting for the egg to drop."

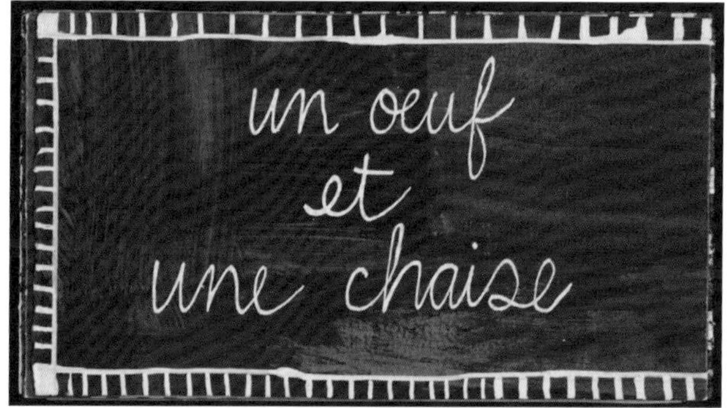


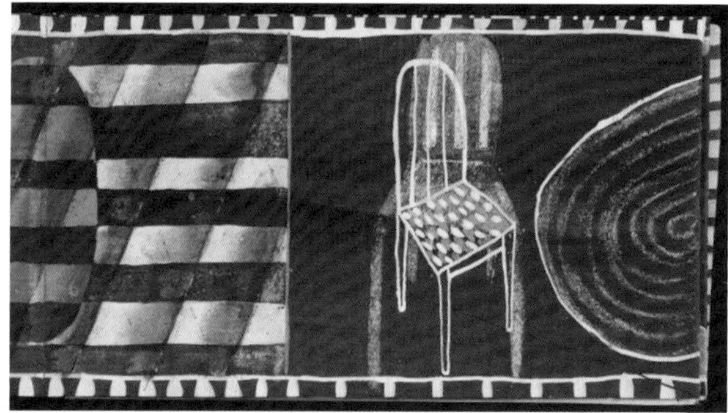

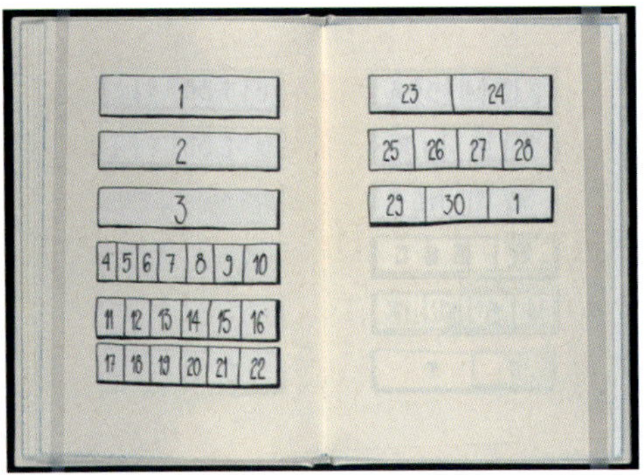


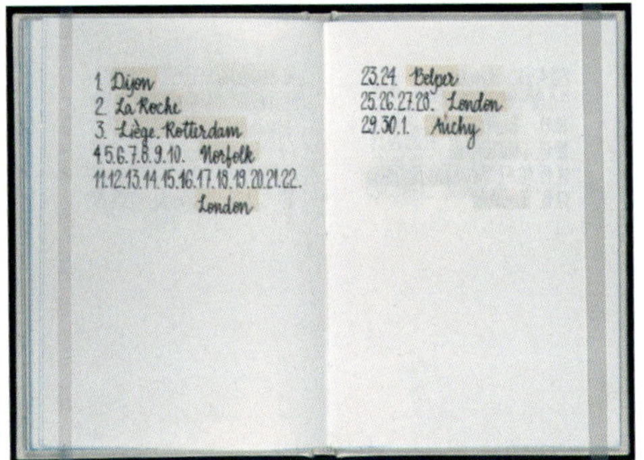


## 1989

Coracle, 1991

A calendar of a sort, on its surface *1989* records Erica Van Horn's travels in 1989; the varied representations of days in the calendar portion of the book correspond with the dates in the index, which indicate where she was on all the days of the year. The visual patterns of the book, both the calendar pages and the dates and location index, are immediately recognizable, and so at first glance, the broad narrative of the book seems obvious. However, a mysterious ratio statement follows the index: 365/231. The index and calendar do not reveal the nature of the 231 days, complicating what seems like a straightforward narrative. In this case, visual patterning both reveals and conceals; a basic narrative is visible but a private narrative is hidden in plain sight. Van Horn underscores the personal and semi-private nature of this calendar-diary by using her own handwriting for both the calendar and the accompanying text.

**La Maison de Ma Soeur a Brulée**
[Onlay], 1984

Of making *La Maison de Ma Soeur a Brulée*, Van Horn has written: "My younger sister was living in Northern New Hampshire. She was managing a condominium complex in a ski resort. I never visited her there. One night there was a huge fire and everything was destroyed. I made the box/book with all of the information I had. I knew she had two friends visiting. I knew there was a swimming pool. I knew that her bird died in the fire. And I knew that she lived in the mountains. The box held the sum total of my knowledge." The effort to contain and process the disturbing event is reflected in the format the artist chose: the work includes five small, heavily-illustrated, concertina-style books housed inside a wooden box.

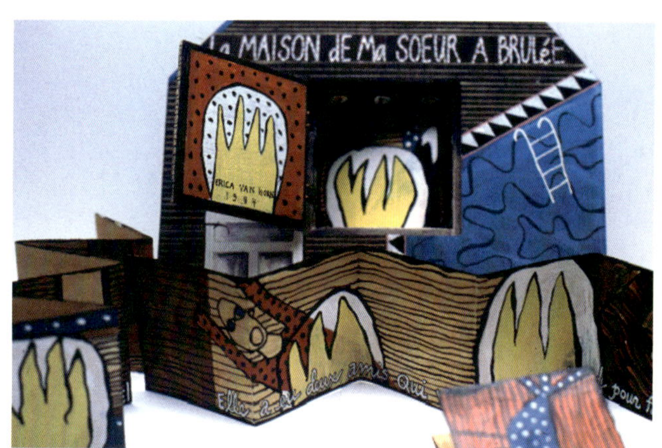

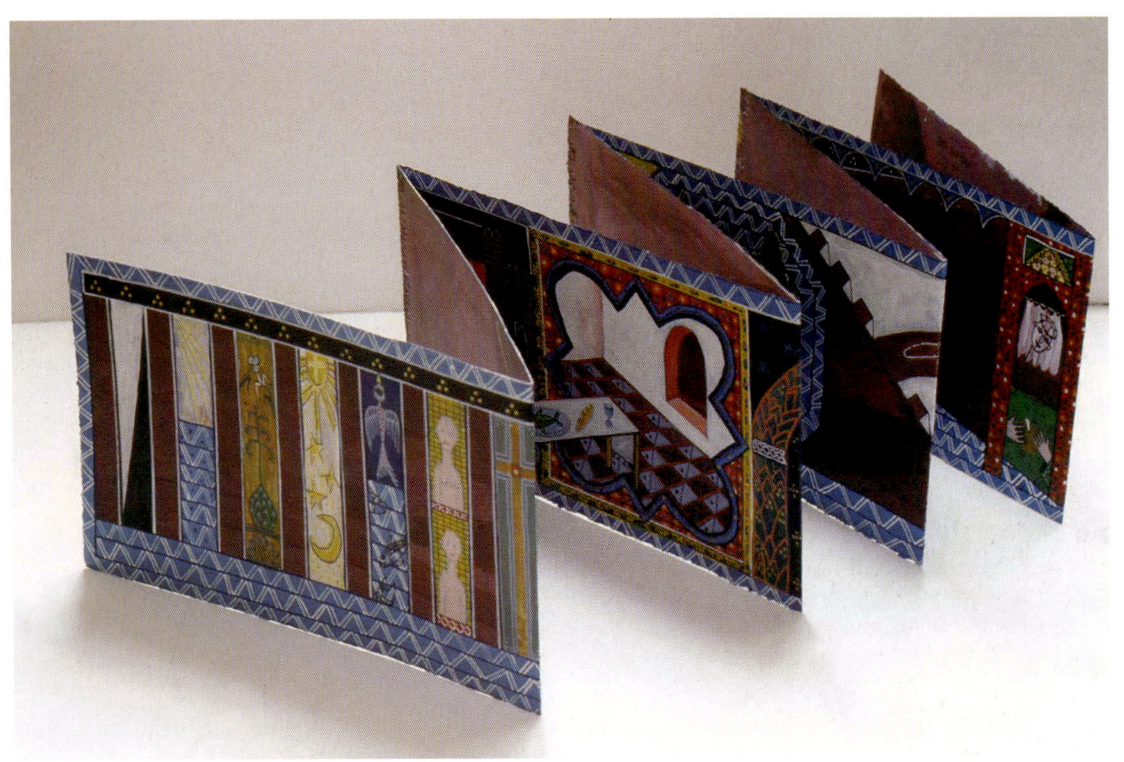

**The Vitry Illuminations**

Vitry-sur-Seine, 1984

While living in an industrial suburb south of Paris, Van Horn traveled frequently to the city to visit museums and observe the city's architecture. When she returned home, she made books that recreated what she'd seen, constructing new arrangements of pattern and texture. "The books were all about reorganizing and representing the imagery I was discovering" the artist writes. Fascinated by the Medieval and Romanesque art she encountered on her Paris trips, Van Horn became interested in the religious symbolism of these periods: "It was fascinating to learn how entire visual vocabularies had evolved. I was mixing it up but still playing with the same vocabulary."

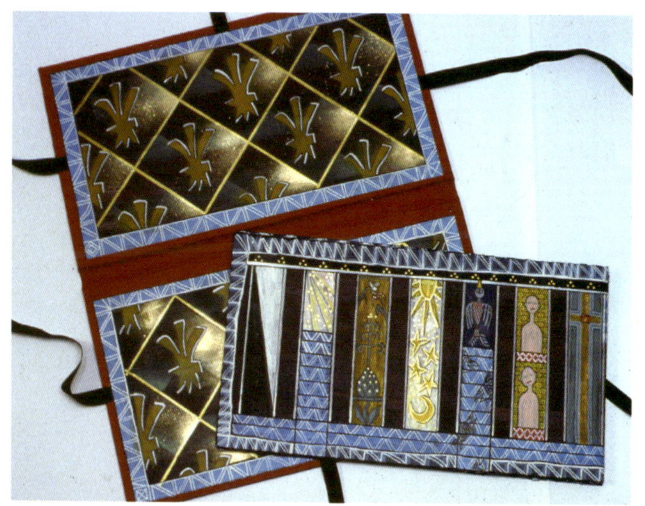

# IDENTITY AND LIKENESS

Much of Erica Van Horn's work is interested in what might be thought of as a kind of portraiture, the creation of imagistic and textual likenesses of both people and places. In various self-portraits, the artist explores the relationship between image and identity, the visual nature of memory, and the perpetual human need to re-imagine the self. Depicting important people and places in her life, she often uses visual metonymy to represent a person indirectly in the figures of closely related objects or words, reducing the idea of *portrait* to its most basic elements. Representations of historic or cultural figures re-narrate and revise well-known stories, layering the artist's impressions or criticisms over the traditional texts. Van Horn's likenesses serve to celebrate and honor their subjects; they reveal something of the artist's relationship to her subject, creating a sense of intimacy and connection for the viewer. Nonetheless, the artist never loses sight of the fact that such artistic representation is evaluative and interpretative; she understands and makes use of the ways portraiture can influence the viewer's broad understanding of its subject.

## An Installation by Erica Van Horn

11 Nov–20 Dec 1986, New York, 1986

A kind of self-portrait, with this postcard announcing an installation of her work at Franklin Furnace in New York in 1986, Van Horn begins to tell the story of her life as an artist. The card refers to books the artist made as a child: in the wake of John F. Kennedy's assassination, she made a book as a way to understand and absorb the traumatic and confusing events of the day. It is easy to recognize in this story many of the distinctive practices and themes that define her oeuvre. For Van Horn, book making has been and remains a means by which one can reflect on, work through, record, narrate, and honor complex experiences, feeling states, and relationships. That the text of the postcard is in her own handwriting reflects both the artist's investment in the imagistic qualities of language and text and her acute awareness of the way handwriting, as a definite and individual marker, can act as a visual representation of its writer.

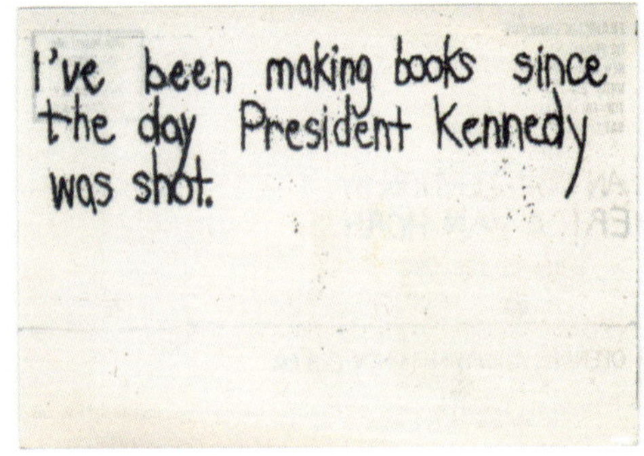


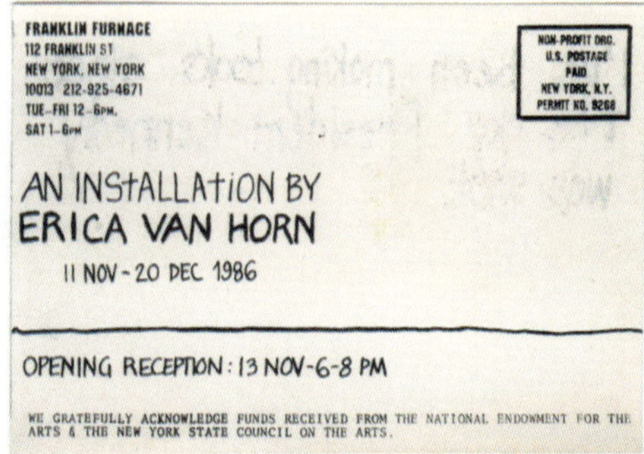

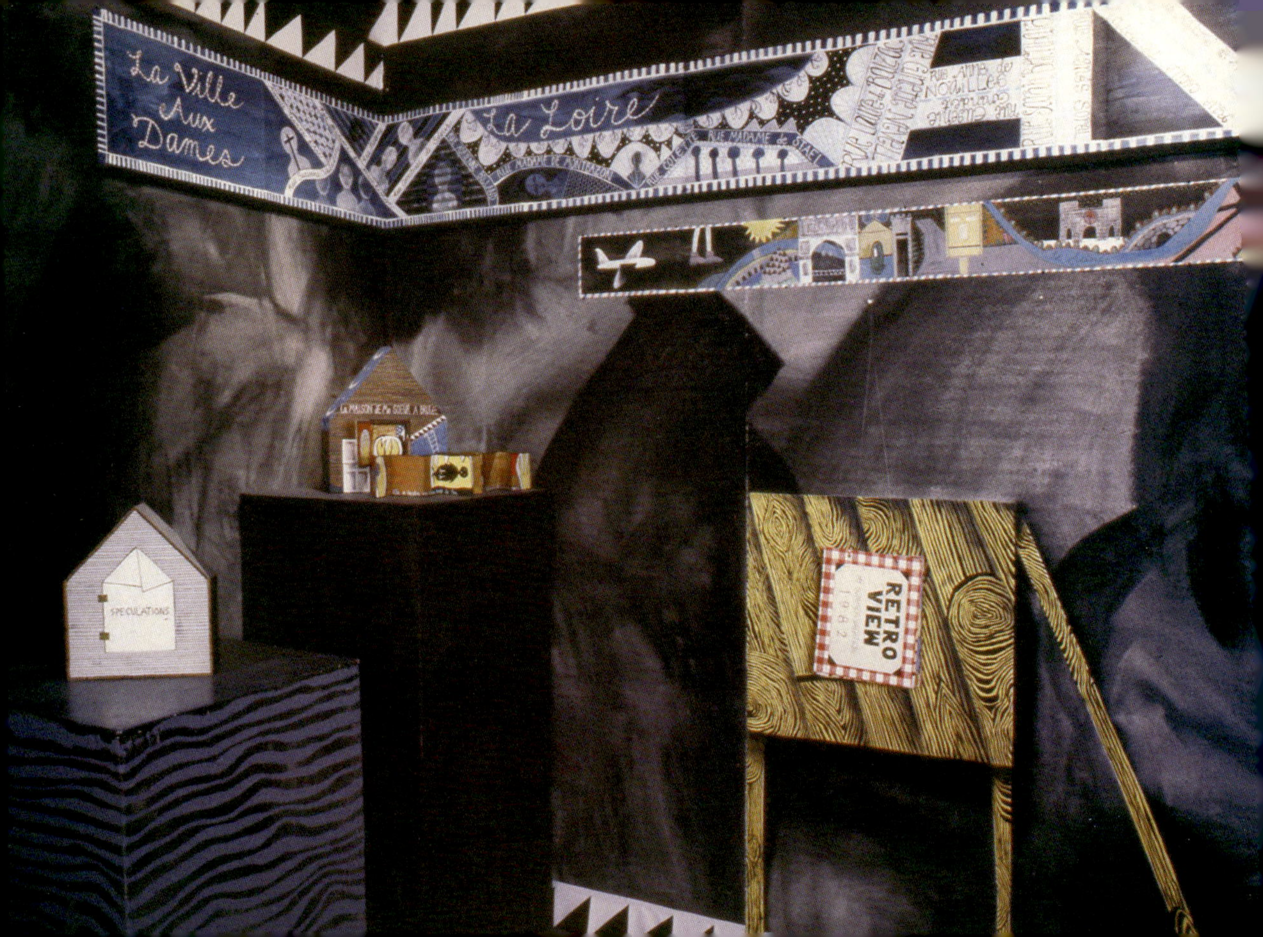
La Ville Aux Dames
La Loire
SPECULATIONS
RETRO VIEW

## Mes Vêtements Sont Souvent Un Problème

France, 1983

One of a series of souvenirs made while Van Horn was living in Paris, the format of this book is modeled on the familiar folders of postcards readily available on the streets of the city: sewn loosely together, a series of cards become an unusual vertical accordion book. *Mes Vêtements Sont Souvent [Une] Un Problème* documents a challenge of the artists' daily life in Paris: "My clothes were ALWAYS a problem (not fashionable, not new, not expensive, and often mismatched)." The clothing depicted here is also visible in other work made during this period, including *Eulogy—Favorite Clothes Who Died in France* 1983, and *Odyssey, Paris* 1982, in which her purple-booted feet can be seen in the first frame.

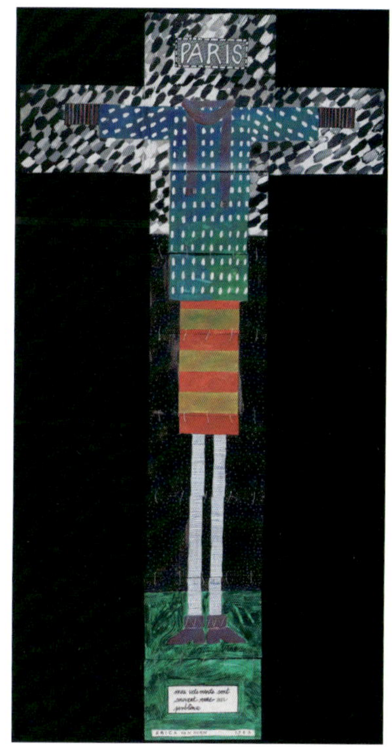

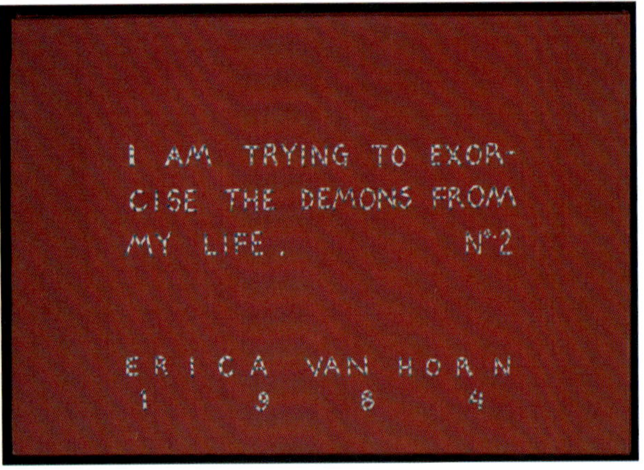


**I am Trying to Exorcise the Demons from My Life, No, 2, 1984**

Paris, 1984

Van Horn made several versions of this book, a self-portrait of the artist by way of her demons, which she refers to as "an oft-repeated attempt to clear my life of negative habits and fears (ie. smoking, drinking, poor health, anxieties, etc.) which impede forward movement." *I am Trying to Exorcise the Demons from My Life* is one of numerous examples where the artist works over an idea again and again, trying to resolve questions of both form and content. Repetition and re-working reveal that many of the subjects she engages in her work are inexhaustible, irresolvable, and thus endlessly fascinating and ripe for continued exploration. "The books bearing this title" she tells us, "served to distract me, but I don't think any demons were exorcised."

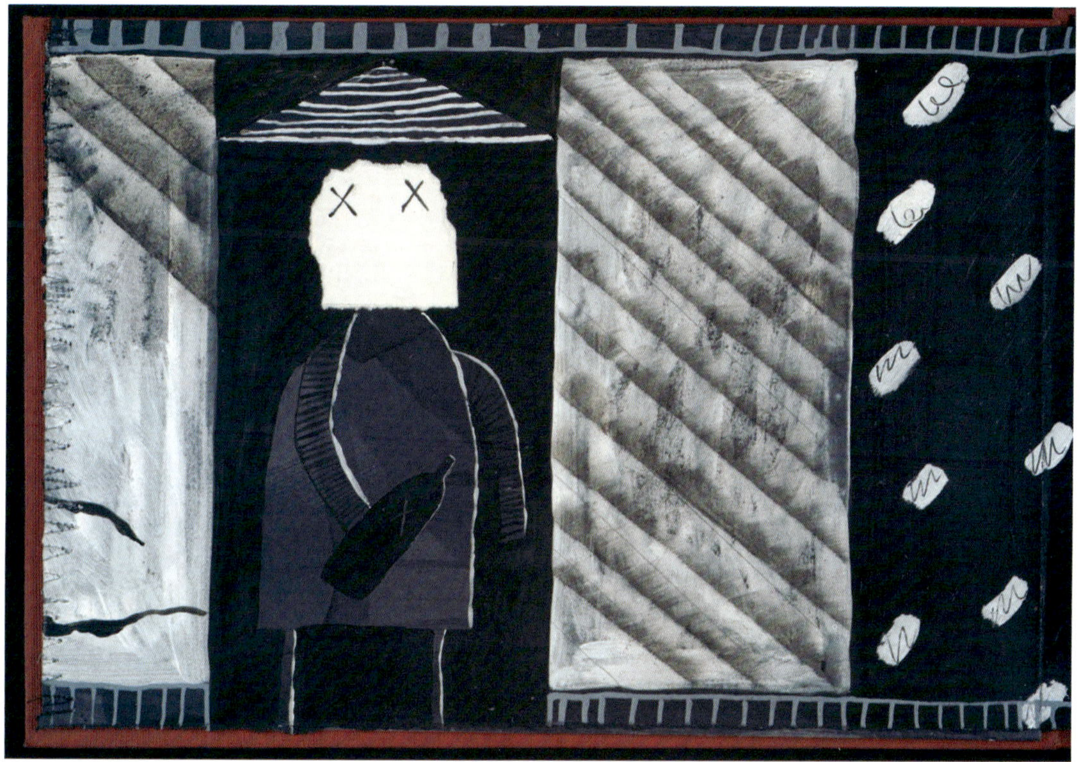

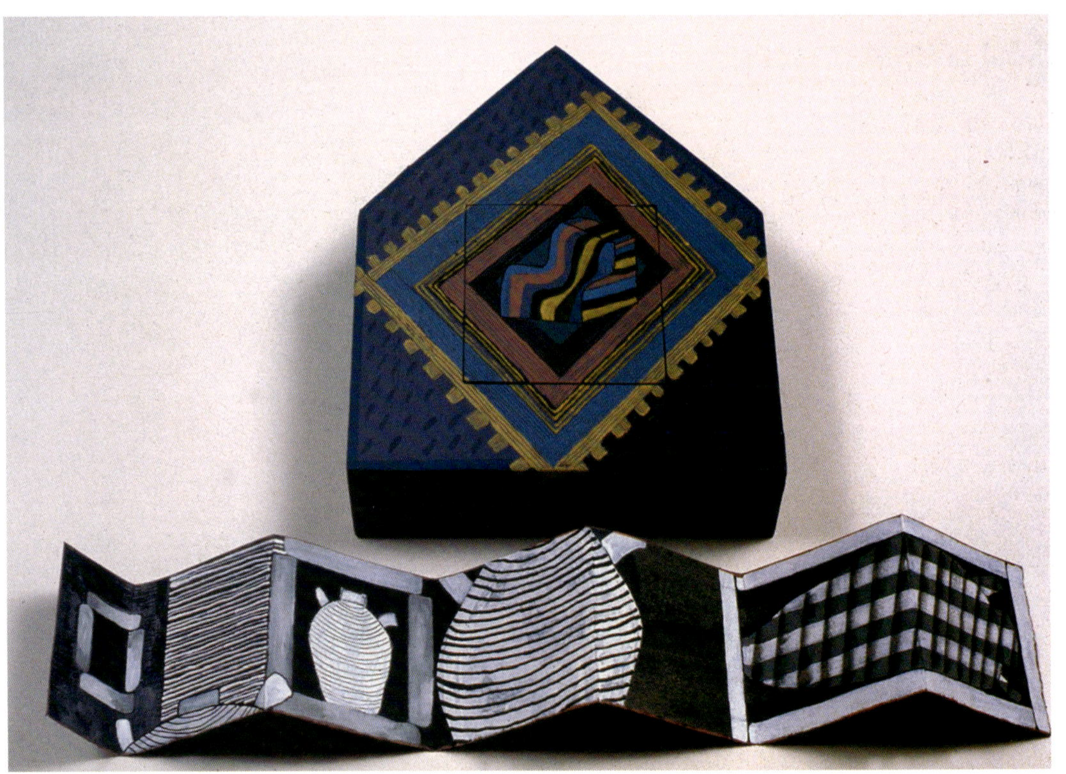

## The Home of Michelle Fekir

Vitry-sur-Seine, 1984

*The Home of Michelle Fekir* documents a friend's home in a housing estate outside of Paris, visually exploring the space in four small concertina-style books housed in a wooden box. In a drab suburb of uniformly built houses, Van Horn was surprised by the dramatic and lively interior of Michelle Fekir's home. Describing the house and her inspiration for this book, she writes: "once inside, the house was all colour. It was full of the fabrics, the pottery and the colours of North Africa. The entire house spiraled in on itself and as one climbed up through it; it was difficult to believe that one was still in this dreary suburb. I thought about Michelle and her house a lot after my visit and eventually made the box to have the colour and energy on the outside and to try to portray the rich patterning and texture of the inside of the house by using only black and white. I hoped that reversing the intensities might say something about appearance versus content."

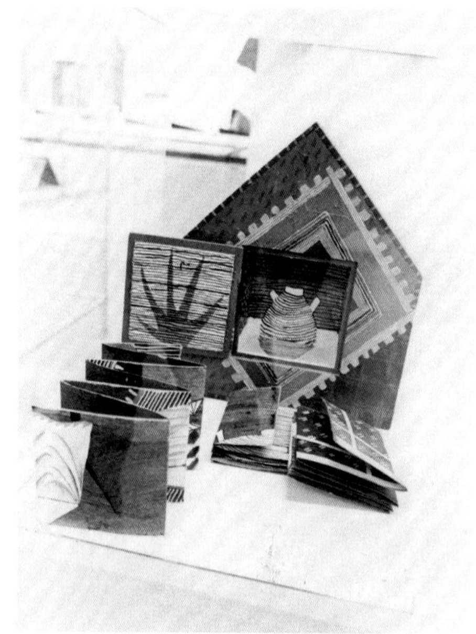

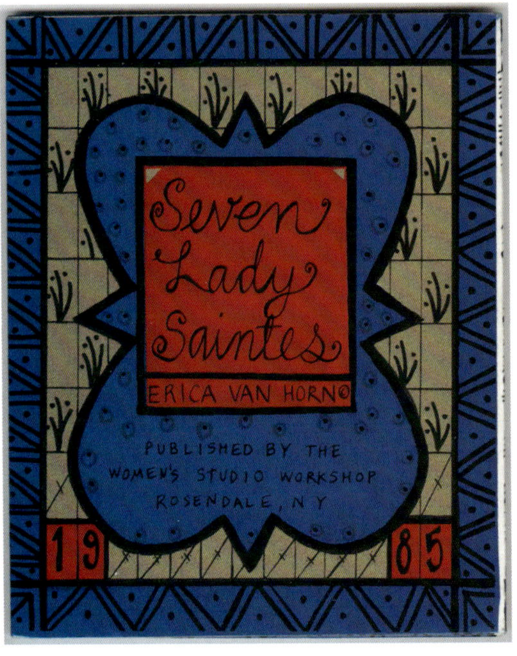


**Seven Lady Saintes**

Rosendale, New York: Women's Studio Workshop, 1985

In this re-imagining of the lives of virgin martyrs from the calendar of Catholic saints, the visual representations are richly decorated and colored in the tradition of Medieval hagiographic art. Short texts reduce the stories of these saints to the essentials, in much the way traditional depictions of Catholic saints narrate their lives through their attributes, the associated objects used to represent the events of their lives. In her lives of the saints, which reveal the sometimes inconsistent and unlikely elements of such stories, the artist calls attention to a tension between portraiture and biography, and between the real and the imagined elements in any historical biography.

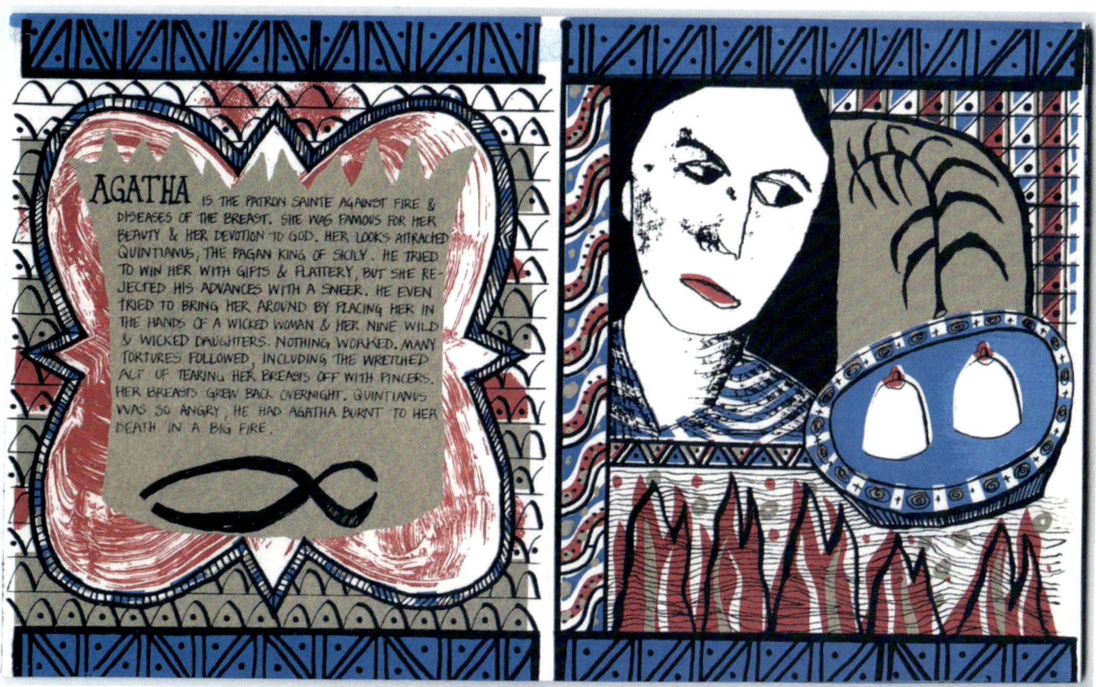
AGATHA IS THE PATRON SAINTE AGAINST FIRE & DISEASES OF THE BREAST. SHE WAS FAMOUS FOR HER BEAUTY & HER DEVOTION TO GOD. HER LOOKS ATTRACTED QUINTIANUS, THE PAGAN KING OF SICILY. HE TRIED TO WIN HER WITH GIFTS & FLATTERY, BUT SHE REJECTED HIS ADVANCES WITH A SNEER. HE EVEN TRIED TO BRING HER AROUND BY PLACING HER IN THE HANDS OF A WICKED WOMAN & HER NINE WILD & WICKED DAUGHTERS. NOTHING WORKED. MANY TORTURES FOLLOWED, INCLUDING THE WRETCHED ACT OF TEARING HER BREASTS OFF WITH PINCERS. HER BREASTS GREW BACK OVERNIGHT. QUINTIANUS WAS SO ANGRY, HE HAD AGATHA BURNT TO HER DEATH IN A BIG FIRE.

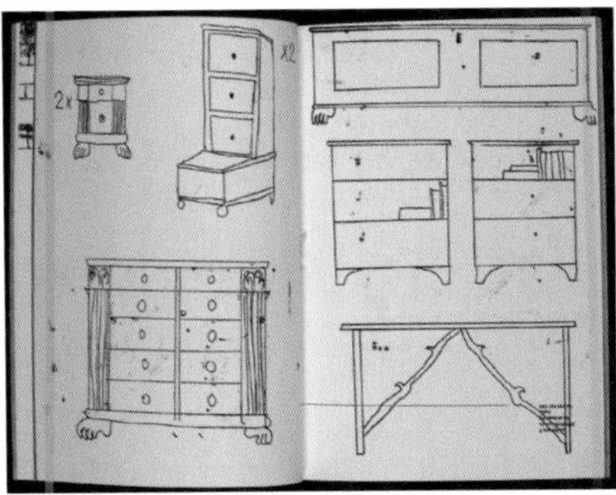

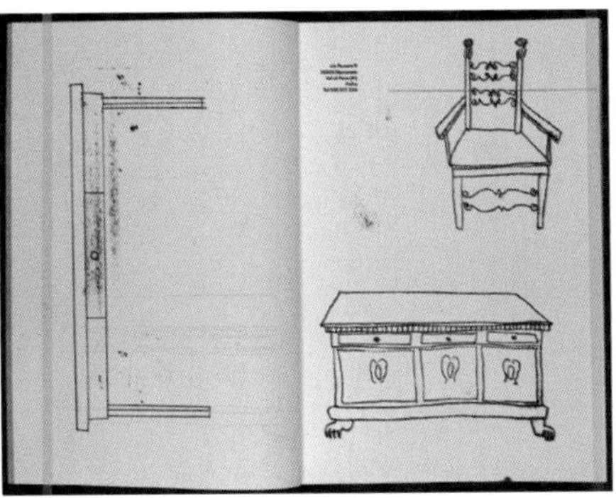

**A Brief Visual Inventory of the Furniture and Objects in the House (Via Perseto 9) which belong to the Goretti Family (as Does the House), June 1990**

Italy, 1991

A collection of line drawings of household articles and furnishings, this book's title accurately describes its contents. The book considers objects out of the context of a room or domestic arrangement, focusing on the particular form of each lamp, table, or chest of drawers. This straightforward act of creating an illustrated catalog of the contents of a home acts as a collective portrait of the Goretti family.

**Small Houses: The Buildings of Tom Browne**
Coracle, 2007

In *Small Houses*, Erica Van Horn celebrates a friend and neighbor. Tom Browne, a retired builder, makes miniature versions of the houses of his friends and family. His work is itself a kind of portraiture, a fact Van Horn recognizes and acknowledges by putting Browne's replica of her own house on the book's cover, essentially making *Small Houses* a sly double portrait. In addition to celebrating Browne's houses, the narrative of *Small Houses* reveals ways in which a maker's sensibility extends to Browne's daily chores and life in rural Tipperary. As part of her *Living Locally* series, *Small Houses* is also a portrait of community and a landscape as viewed through the work of one member, recorded and described by another.

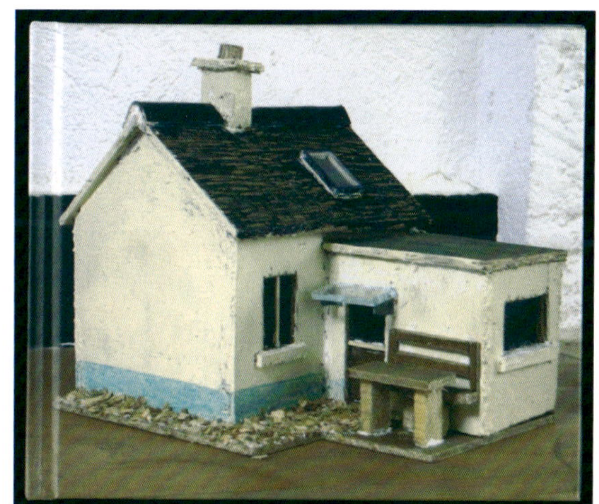

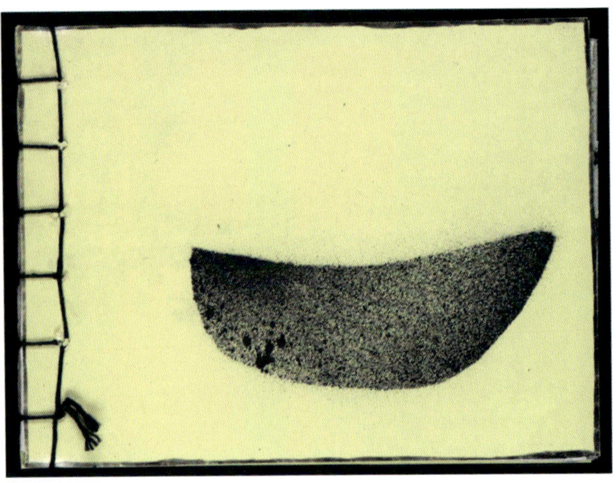

**Simon (1st century), Apostle: Called either the Canaanite or the Zealot**

Docking, 1989

A mixture of handwritten and printed texts and drawings, this unique book celebrates October 28, the feast of Saint Simon. Van Horn uses text from a dictionary of the lives of the saints and drawings of Simon and his common attributes, a boat and a book, repeating and reconfiguring these simple elements to highlight the fact that the subject of the portrait is not only Saint Simon, but also her husband and collaborator, fellow artist Simon Cutts. Cutts is well known as a book maker, and together the couple run a literary and art press, Coracle, which takes its name from a kind of small boat very like those depicted in the drawings for this book.

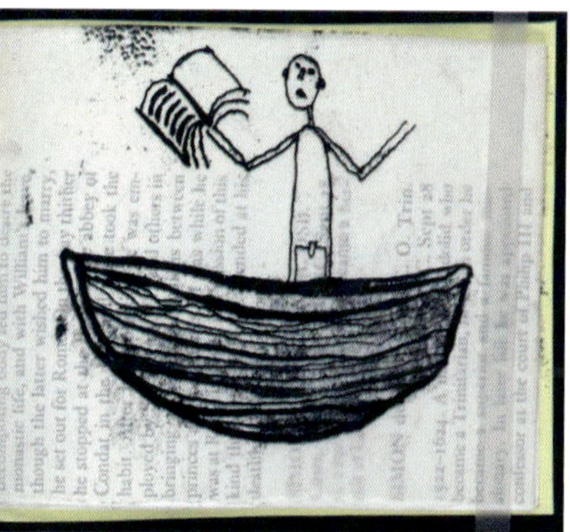
further. In art Simon's usu
a boat, as on East Anglia
or without a book), or else
ich according to the traditio
by the *Golden Legend*, was th
which the heathen priest
o death. In the East the feas
1 July, the traditional date

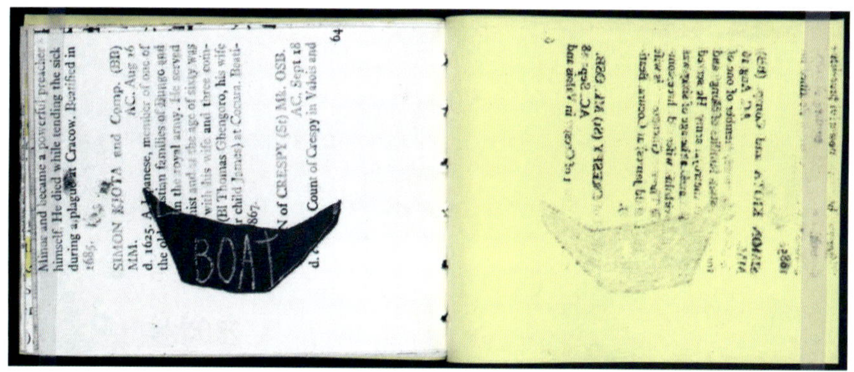
Minor and became a powerful preacher
himself. He died while tending the sick
during a plague at Cracow. Beatified in
1685.
SIMON KIOTA and Comp. (BB)
MM. AC. Aug 16
N of CRESPY (St) Mr. OSB.
AC. Sept 18
Count of Crespy in Valois and
BOAT

# CHRONOLOGY OF BOOKS & CARDS

fc: folded card, pc: postcard

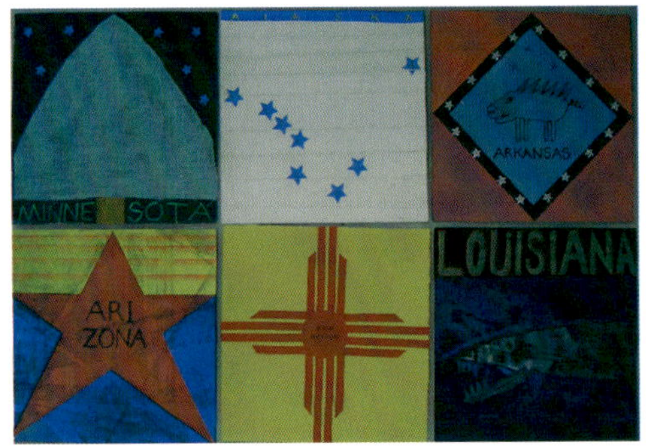


1979

**Never Marry a Man of this Type**
pc, silkscreen
**Celestial Horizon**
pc, silkscreen

1981

**Your United States**
53pp unbound, acrylic and mixed media on Arches, 260 x 260 each, clamshell box, buckram over boards with acrylic, 300 x 300 x 100 (*left*)
**Abe Sada** by Sekeine Hiroshi
66pp, handwritten text with 9 illustrations, mixed media on grey fabriano, case bound with raised image on cover, 250 x 180

1982

**The Importance of Being Ernst (Max)**
40pp, collage, acrylic, casebound, buckram over boards, 150 x 100 x 30
**Speculations**
(Edition of 3, each wooden house different)
Acrylic and wood-burning on house shaped box, 160 x 130 x 55, door with leather hinges, 9 folders inside the door cavity, collaged image inside each folder, image size: 90 x 90, typewritten texts

**Retro-View: My Summer Vacation**
22pp, acrylic, postcards, mixed materials on board, ring binders, 220 x 260

**Souvenir No.9: Cats**
Seven cards, acrylic with stitching, 1070 x 100 open, in folder of card, 160 x 100

## 1983

**Je Ne Parle Pas Française**
acrylic and chalk on 16 squares of card mounted in folder, acrylic on buckram over boards with ribbon closures, 470 x 525 open, 470 x 260

**Une Oeuf et Une Chaise**
11pp concertina, machine stitching, acrylic and chalk on Arches paper, 140 x 260, in folder: acrylic on buckram over boards with ribbon closures, 150 x 275

**Scraps of An Aborted Collaboration** (first state)
8pp, acrylic and pencil on Arches paper, Japanese stab binding, 110 x 110

**Gothic No.1**
12pp concertina with machine stitching, acrylic on Arches paper, 150 x 2540 open, in folder: old chair seat leather on buckram over boards with ribbon ties, 160 x 275

**Gothic No.2**
12pp concertina with machine stitching, acrylic on Arches paper, 150 x 2540 open, in folder: old chair seat leather on buckram over boards with ribbon ties, 160 x 275

**Speculations**
Contained in a house-shaped box, *Speculations* considers the unusual language used to describe real estate. "Terms like INVEST IN SAND caught my attention, and I couldn't stop thinking about it. Each of the folders inside the box offers the option of a dream life, all in a realtors' language." As is the case with several other projects from this period, *Speculations* was made in several variant copies; each copy was enclosed in a different house-like box.

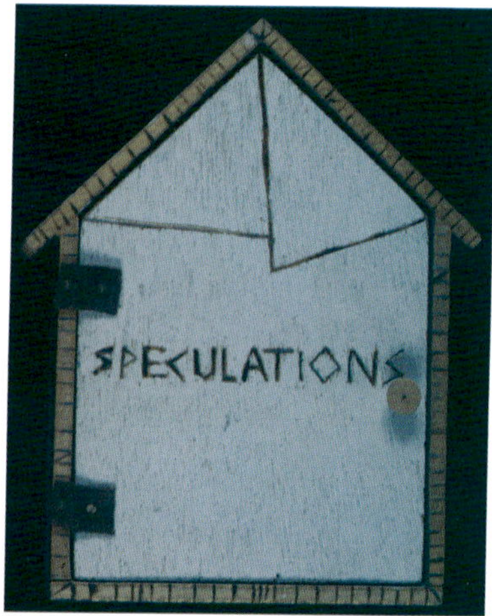

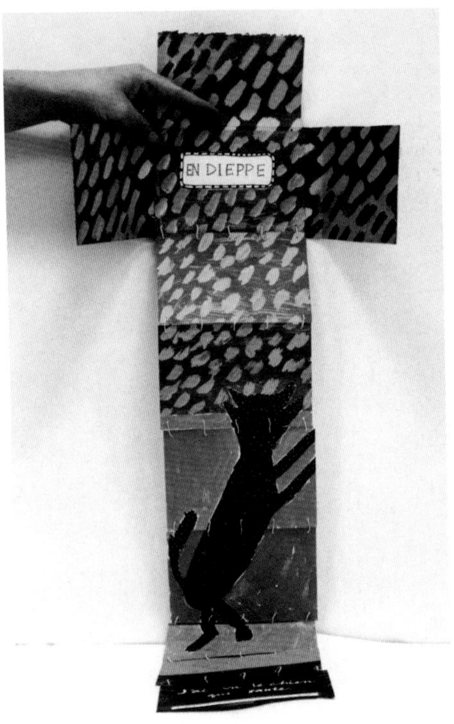


**La Maison de Michelle Fekir**
Acrylic paint on wooden house-shaped box, with hinged door, 320 x 290 x 65, 4 concertinas inside, acrylic and chalk on Arches paper

**Souvenir No.16: Mes Vêtements sont Souvent un Problème**
8 cards with connecting hand stitches in a folder (vertical concertina), acrylic on card with stabbed holes, 900 x 460, open, card folder with acrylic and labels, 110 x 170

**Souvenir No.17 Orly**
nine postcards of airplanes with acrylic, connecting stitches, (vertical concertina), 1030 x 440 open, card folder with acrylic and labels, 110 x 170

**Souvenir No.18: (En Dieppe) J'ai Vu Le Chien Qui Saute**
8pp, connected with thread stitches, acrylic on card, 920 x 420 open, card folder, 110 x 170 (left)

**I Restrict Myself to Eight Favorite Things a Day**
9pp each day, unbound, acrylic on Arches paper, 310 x 230, in yellow folder, buckram over boards: each day with different coloured folders, 320 x 240

**Reference Book No.1**
26pp, ink on pages with offset borders, Japanese stab binding, buckram over boards with acrylic, 220 x 325

**Creation/Perfection**
6 panel concertina, acrylic and chalk on paper, mounted onto boards, buckram, ribbon closures, 150 x 920 open, 150 x 150

**Illuminated Books No.1**
(little standing saint with letter O)
acrylic on 6 book spines, books drilled and held together with string, 250 x 180 x 230

**Reference File of Envelopes Received December 1983–December 1996**
154 books of envelopes sewn together, approximately 260 x 180 each, covers of various materials, acrylic or ink, with Japanese stab bindings, contained in six boxes, 210 x 310 x 300 each

**Favorite Clothes Who Died in France**
16pp, acrylic on pages made of striped denim backed by corduroy, machine sewn. Japanese stab binding, 190 x 230

**Choisissez-Vous**
10pp, concertina, acrylic, photographs on card, 65 x 360 open, in small metal oval tin with acrylic, 75 x 50 x 10

**Pour La Plupart, Je ne Comprends pas Les Conversations Francaises**
42pp, acrylic and ink on paper, correction strips from golf ball typewriter, Japanese stab binding, 100 x 150

**La Ville Aux Dames** (one of three versions of different size)
12 panel concertina, machine stitched, folded into buckram covered boards with ribbon ties, acrylic on Arches paper, 280 x 2104 open

**Animated Architectural Details in a Cheesebox**
12 cards, chalk and acrylic, 85 x 85, wooden cheesebox with painted label, 100 x 100 x 30

Creation Perfection

*Creation Perfection* reinterprets religious iconography using the repetition of one visual element—the hand—to represent the Six Elements of the Catholic tradition: Divine Power, Majesty, Wisdom, Love, Mercy, Justice. The accordion book format allows for different ways of physically "reading" and understanding the book—page by page, viewing the Elements in discrete pairs, or open to reveal the six images in a single, linear form.

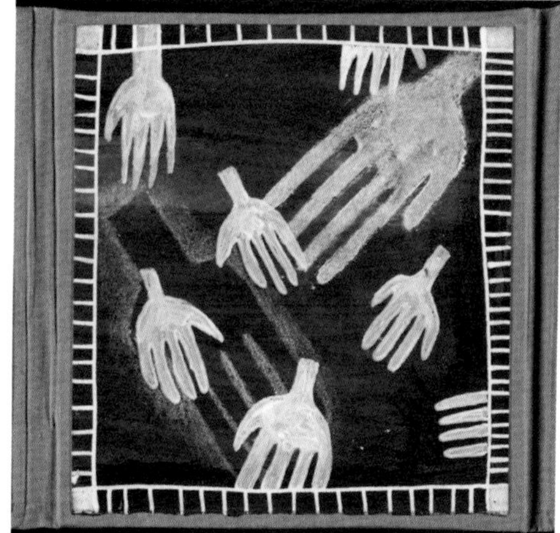

**Favorite Clothes Who Died in France**

A literal exploration of the meeting of form and content, *Eulogy—Favorite Clothes that Died in France* takes as its raw materials the clothes referred to in the book's title. On pages made of purple corduroy and green denim, the book has painted images of various articles of clothing which "died" while living in Paris. The book is both whimsical and witty, but the clothes in *Eulogy* are also a curious preoccupation, recurring throughout the work of the period. *Eulogy* embodies key themes in the work, including identity and self-portraiture and the basic elements of narrative; the book also exhibits material and structural elements that remain significant throughout the body of her work, such as the reuse of found materials and the use of hand and machine stitching.

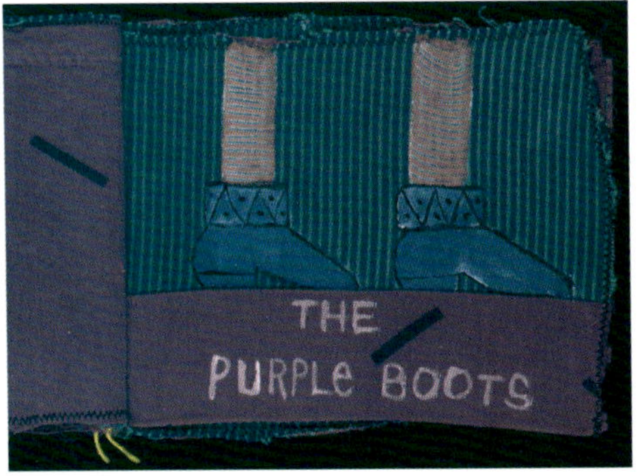


**Odyssey: Paris 1982–1983**
12pp concertina, acrylic on Arches paper, 140 x 2800 open, in folder, buckram over boards with ribbon ties, 150 x 245

## 1984

**Scraps of an Aborted Collaboration** (2nd state)
16pp, 140 x 220

**Jewels I have Loved** (2nd state)
26pp, 280 x 220

**Priorities**
22pp, 210 x 300

**He Wears Green Shoes**
22pp, 210 x 300

**Le Moyen Age**
26pp, 300 x 210

**Doomed to a Life of Compulsive Meaninglessness**
22pp, 210 x 300, photocopy with Japanese stab binding, unnumbered

**I am Trying to Exorcise the Demons in my Life No.1**
8pp concertina, acrylic and chalk on Arches paper, machine stitching, end pages glued into covers, 380 x 3100 open, acrylic on red buckram over boards, 380 x 399

**I am Trying to Exorcise the Demons From My Life No.2**
8pp concertina, acrylic and chalk on Arches paper, machine stitching, end pages glued into covers, 269 x 2950 open, red buckram over boards, 280 x 370

**I am Trying to Exorcise the Demons in My Life No.3**
8pp concertina, acrylic and chalk on Arches paper, machine stitching, end pages glued into covers, 180 x 1600 open, black buckram over boards, 180 x 190
**I Am Trying to Exorcise The Demons in My Life No.4**
8pp concertina, acrylic and chalk on Arches paper, machine stitching, end pages glued into covers, 269 x 2950 open, black buckram over boards, 280 x 370
**Working Notes in a Cheesebox**
12pp, acrylic on card, 110 x 110 each, in wooden cheesebox with painted label, 120 x 120 x30
**Luzillé (Village Portrait, Val du Loire)**
8pp, concertina with machine stitching, acrylic on Arches paper, 385 x 1430 open, in folder of buckram over boards with ribbon ties, 395 x 200
**Guy on Stage**
14pp, paper over boards containing monoprints, photographs, and acrylic, buckram over boards with Japanese stab binding using thick black string, 240 x 310 x 40
**Eins. Zwei. Drei.**
3 small books, 16pp, monoprints on painted Arches paper, Japanese stab binding, 60 x 95 each
**Random Retable**
3 panels, acrylic on wood, with buckram hinges, 610 x 1040 standing open
**Moyen Age III**
8pp, acrylic on Arches paper, concertina with machine stitching, 195 x 360 each page, 195 x 2850 open, in buckram folder with ribbon ties
**Moyen Age No.IV**
10pp, acrylic on Arches paper, concertina with machine stitching, in buckram over boards folder with ribbon ties, 220 x 325
**The Vitry Illuminations**
8pp, acrylic on Arches paper, concertina with sewing machine stitching, 195 x 360, each page, 195 x 2850 open, in buckram folder with ribbon ties
**Jewels I Have Loved**
6pp, acrylic on Arches paper, mounted on concertina of board and buckram, 310 x 190 x 30 closed, 310 x 1145 open
**25. Avenue Anatole France (& the Neighborhood)**
20pp, ink on paper with printed offset borders, buckram over boards with acrylic, Japanese stab binding, 220 x 325
**Illuminated Books No.2** (snake/gargoyle in the letter S)
acrylic on 5 book spines, drilled together with string, 200 x 180 x 150
**Illuminated Books No.3** (Saints Head with red patterned background)
acrylic on 5 book spines, 260 x 200 x 200
**The New Woman (illustrated) 7 April–4 July 1984**
320pp, acrylic and ink drawings in existing book of that title, 240 x 160 x 35

**Ants in Space**
acrylic on circular wooden box with hinged door, 329 x 340 x 65, 4 booklets inside, acrylic and chalk on Arches paper, 2pp, mounted into folders of buckram covered boards, 190 x 80 each (*below*)
**Seven Lady Saintes**
(2 states: one version with red buckram and one with grey buckram) 6pp, acrylic on Arches paper, mounted into concertina of buckram over board, 310 x 1145 open, 310 x 190 x 30

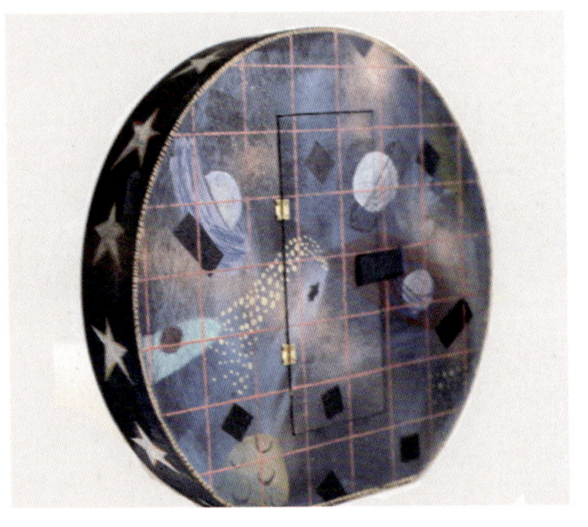

**Some Words From That Letter** (first state)
32pp, acrylic and ink on Arches paper, Japanese stab binding, 110 x 160
**La Maison de Ma Soeur a Brulée**
Acrylic on wooden house-shaped box, hinged door, 320 x 290 x 65, containing 5 concertinas, acrylic and chalk on Arches paper
**Ten Portraits (After Arnulf Rainer)**
22pp, acrylic on Arches paper, Japanese stab binding, 130 x 140

## 1985

**Seven Lady Saintes**
16 panels (240 x 210 each), silkscreen concertina in stitched plastic envelope with fiberglass grid, and Velcro fastener, 90 signed and numbered copies, Women's Studio Workshop, Rosendale, NY
**Menses Dorchester (Stations of the Curse)**
26pp, acrylic and ink on paper, Japanese stab binding, 280 x 380
**The New Man**
unknown pp, acrylic, ink and pencil drawings in existing book, 245 x 160 x 34
**15 Men in a Book**
30pp, acrylic on pink office paper, plastic cover with acrylic title, office binding, 280 x 220

**Bookcase Study for Installation at Franklin Furnace, 1985**
This study documents plans for an installation of work; parts of the image were painted directly on a sliding wooden door at the gallery, making it possible to represent books that were not included in the show by their titles. Several of the noted books, including *Odyssey, Seven Lady Saintes, Seven Virtues and Seven Liberal Arts*, are illustrated in the present volume.

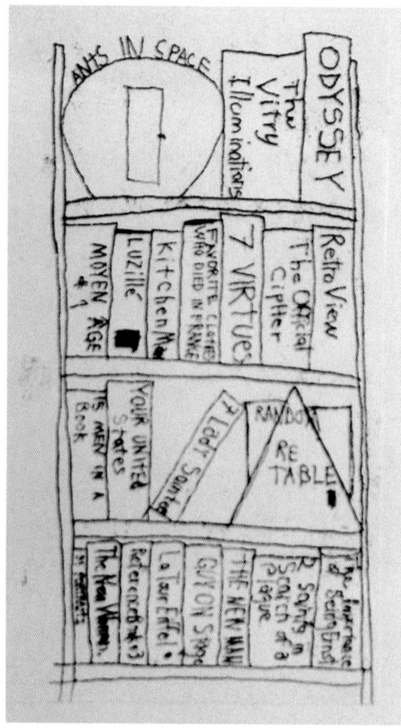


**Two Saints in Search of a Plague**
4pp, acrylic on Arches paper on buckram covered boards, concertina, 330 x 1040 open
**Some Words from that Letter**
255 x 255 x 65 painted wooden box with hinged door, 5 concertina booklets inside, 65 x 600 each, acrylic on paper
**The Seven Virtues**
9pp, acrylic on Arches paper, concertina, 360 x 3110, in cover, buckram over boards ribbon closures, 370 x 370
**Illuminated Books: Reparata**
acrylic on 5 books spines,held together with string, 190 x 200 x 140
**Illuminated Books: Agatha**
acrylic on 5 books spines held together with string, 190 x 240 x 140
**Illuminated Books: Demon Taking Hold**
Acrylic on 5 book spines, held together with string through drilled books, 200 x 240 x 200

**Illuminated books: Chateau Saint**
Acrylic on 5 book spines, held together with string through the drilled books, 190 x 250 x 140
**Illuminated Book: Feet of a Saint**
Acrylic on 6 book spines, held together with string through the drilled books, 195 x 250 x 140

## 1986

**Demon Dancing**
One pc in boxed set of postcards in folder, letterpress, signed and numbered, Purgatory Pie, NYC
**Moi, Je Déteste BHV**
224pp, cut up catalogue from the Bazaar Hotel de Ville department store in Paris, Japanese stab binding with string loop to hang it up. acrylic on covers, 40 x 110
**Black Dog White Bark**
2nd state(painted) with Louis Asekoff
24pp, acrylic and enamel paint on leftover cards from an exhibition in Norway, Japanese stab binding, 210 x 120
**Abe Sada**
(boxed version) by Sekeine Hiroshi
51 unbound pages, ink and acrylic on Arches paper, 305 x 380, in clamshell box, buckram over boards, 335 x 420 x 50
**Demons Plague Me. Daily**
30pp, acrylic and monoprints on Arches paper, Japanese stab binding, 220 x 280
**Pictures of Someone Else's Family**
18pp, found photographs, metal stitches, Japanese stab binding with acrylic paint, 100 x 170
**Random Pictures of a Sporting Event**
14pp, found photographs, metal stitches, Japanese stab binding, with acrylic paint,100 x 170
**Someone Else's Vacation**
22pp, found photographs with covers made of envelopes, Japanese stab binding with acrylic paint 105 x 165
Book hanging, with a string, from upper right hand corner of framed colour photograph 350 x 490
**On Fruit and Vegetable Bags, 31 Portraits, Self and Projected, One a Day, May 1986**
66pp, acrylic, ink, crayon on paper bags, covers made of bags also, Japanese stab binding, 280 x 240
**The Yellow Wood-Grained Table**
4 panel concertina, acrylic on Arches, each page mounted on buckram covered boards, 230 x 145, 230 x 595 open
**Official Cipher**
120pp, drawings in Masonic cipher book, blue leatherette cover, approx. 130 x 75

## 1987

**Black Dog White Bark**
with Louis Asekoff
32pp offset, with Japanese stab binding, 210 x 130, 200 copies, Visual Studies Workshop, Rochester, NY

**Sentences to Think About**
24pp, monoprint texts on paper, Japanese stab binding, 240 x 310
**Illuminated Books No.20: The Feet of A Saint**
acrylic on 4 book spines drilled and tied, 240 x 190 x 165

## 1988

**Eighty Nine Women Drawn in a Book**
10 February1987–1 February 1988, 156pp, mixed media in found accountancy ledger (columnar book) 330 x 390 x 20
**Illuminated books No. 18 : Demon Tumbling Down Stairs**
acrylic on 5 book spines, books wired together through two holes drilled in the middle, 240 x 200 x 160
**The Transparent Year**
24pp, ink on tracing paper, Japanese stab binding, 295 x 210
**Collection 25 + 25**
100pp, newsprint photographs pasted in, ink. paper covers, with glued text, photograph and acrylic, both sides of book serve as the cover, 210 x 210

## 1989

**No Rice or Confetti on the steps or inside**
with Simon Cutts, marriage announcement
4pp, letterpress and rubber stamp, folded and stitched in envelope, 150 x 90, 200 copies
**Simon (1st century) Apostle**
28pp, photocopy, acrylic, ink on several kinds of paper, with yellow vinyl covers, stab binding, 110 x 150
**Italian Lesson No.1**
Postcard with bw photo, rubber stamp, 62 copies

## 1990

**Jewels I Have Loved**
28p, letterpress in 7 colours, casebound, 185 x 170, 200 signed and numbered copies, Coracle
**187 interjections from the second half of the talk by Dennis Adams together with 12 summations by Roger Took**
2 small booklets, 105 x 75 each (14pp and 12pp) in folder, photocopy, sewn, 200 copies, Coracle
**Sans Signaux**
with Simon Cutts
24pp, letterpress in four colours, sewn and casebound, 260 x 290, 100 signed and numbered copies, Coracle
**Italian Lessons No. 2 & 3: Disposal Bag**
Laminated paper folder with 2 disposal bags and rubber stamp, letterpress 280 x 185, 100 copies
**Italian Lesson No. 4**
36pp, recycled notes, sewn, 75 x 50, 66 copies
**Italian Lesson no. 5: La Pelle Rossa**
pc, red leather, rubber stamps, 99 copies
**Stoppage**
with Simon Cutts
Letterpress print, 2 colours with hole cut, 250 x 270, 4 signed and numbered copies

**Jewels I Have Loved**
Both an album of lost pieces of jewelry and an elegy for a lost friend. Line drawings of a cameo, bracelet, and several lost earrings appear alongside short descriptions of their significance and where and when each went missing. The final text describes the life and death of a childhood friend and meditates on the relationships of grief and memory to physical objects; "I look all day" Van Horn writes, "to find myself in the things I touch."

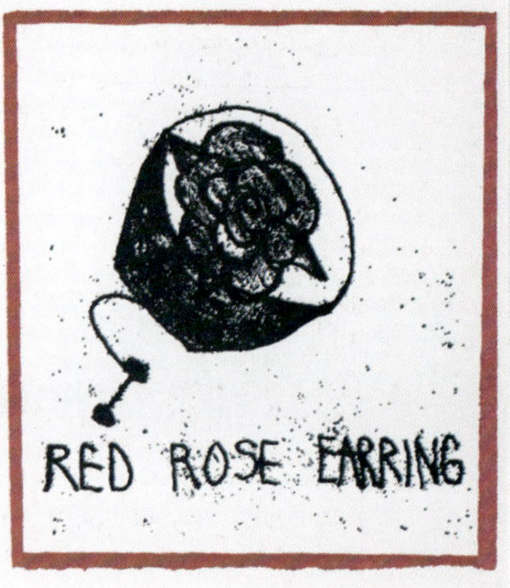


## 1991

**Italian Lesson No. 6: Argo**
24pp, offset with sewn on wrappers and labels glued in, 150 x 130, 200 copies, Coracle

**Change of Address card**
pc, rubber stamps

**Happy Picnics in Snowdrop Time**
with Simon Cutts for the New Year 1991
fc, photocopy and letterpress, 125 x 180, 200 copies

**A Brief Visual Inventory of the furniture and objects in the house (Via Perseto 9) Which belong to the Goretti family, (as does the house) June 1990**
36pp, photocopy, perfect bound with wrappers, 290 x 210, 25 signed and numbered copies

**1989**
56pp, offset in 2 colours, casebound, 185 x 130, 200 numbered copies, Coracle

**The Importance of Being Ian Hamilton Finlay**
37pp concertina, envelopes machine-stitched together, with ink and rubber stamps, in clamshell box, buckram over boards, printed text on inside of box, 280 x 15540

**Lumieres label**
wine label, photocopied

1992

**Italian Lesson no. 7: The Addresses of James Joyce and Nora Barnacle in Trieste**
fc, letterpress, 140 x 115 in printed envelope, 200 copies, Coracle
**Italian Lessons 8 & 9 & 10: Companions and Menus**
with Simon Cutts
56pp, 4-colour offset, letterpress, rubber stamps and photocopy, casebound, paper over boards, 181 x 130, 250 numbered copies, Coracle
**Aglio 6 Olio**
with Simon Cutts
156pp, letterpress and photocopy, casebound, 76 x 76, 200 numbered copies in cardboard box. Coracle
**Chasniers label**
fc, letterpress with thermographed label, 130 x 120, 70 numbered copies
**Antwerp Airport**
28pp, photocopy on hand-painted pages, casebound, 150 x 130, 35 numbered copies, Coracle
**Skegness Rock**
fc, offset, 100 x 100, Coracle
**Lumieres 1990**
wine label, photocopy
**Business Card** (for *Companions and Menus*)
**Business Card** (for *Italian Lessons*)

1993

**Le Poet (for the New year 1993)** with Simon Cutts
fc, colour xerox
**A Paint Peeling**
fc (see *Two Peelings*, 2004)
**Italian Lesson No.11: In Italy One Is Only Allowed Eleven Words Per Postcard**
pc, letterpress, 300 copies, workfortheeyetodo, London
**Italian Lesson no.12: Venetien Blinds**
fc in Printed envelope, letterpress and fake photograph (photocopy, cut with deckle edge), 185 x 160
**Boy Bell's Book of Envelope Interiors** (1st state)
24pp, photocopy and tipped-in examples, 150 x 150, sewn, 50 copies, Coracle
**Stiles and the Pennine Way**
4pp, offset in 3 colours, and hand colouring, letterpress, casebound with ribbon ties, 360 x 235, 100 numbered copies, Coracle
**Water of Recess**
with Simon Cutts
Boxed glass flask filled with river water and sewn booklet in cardboard box, 100 x 40 x 35, 30 numbered copies, Coracle
**Envelope Interior Reference File 1993–2007**
522 cards, cards printed letterpress with tipped-in samples of envelope interiors, each card 180 x 180, in buckram covered box, 225 x 200 x 365

## 1994

**Scraps of an Aborted Collaboration**
18pp, offset in 3 colours, Japanese stab binding, 200 x 113, 200 numbered copies, Coracle
**Forty Fungi**
with Harry Gilonis
90pp, offset, casebound, 210 x 113, 200 copies, Coracle
**Marmalade Card**
pc, Form card No.21, photocopy
**Muker Literary Institute List**
pc, Form Card No.29
**the irish harp is not constructed but carved out of a single tree like a canoe**
with Simon Cutts
letterpress folder containing 4 section concertina, 100 x 760, Coracle (at Irish Museum of Modern Art)
**Boy Bell's Book of Envelope Interiors** (3rd state)
24pp, photocopy and tipped-in examples, 150 x 150, sewn, 100 copies, Coracle
**A Waffle for 1994**
with Simon Cutts, New Year card
4pp, letterpress and offset, 130 x 155, Coracle
**Italian lesson No.13 : Identificazione**
10 panel concertina, letterpress, rubber stamp, finger print ink, 80 x 51, in plastic sleeve, 80 x 512 open, 200 copies
**Lumieres label** with light bulb pattern
wine label, photocopy
**A Swale Walk**
pc, Muker card announcement

## 1995

**Docking Competitions**
with Laurie Clark
48pp, offset in 2 colours, casebound, 107 x 150, 200 copies, Coracle
**Italian Lesson No.14: People are Bueno not Bene**
pc, letterpress, 300 copies, workfortheeyetodo, London
**Envelope Interiors 2** (Pink volume)
288pp, photocopy with tipped-in envelope interiors, casebound, in slipcase, 155 x 160, 9 numbered copies
**Invite for *Forty Fungi* launch**
pc, Form Card No.40
**Envelope Interior Calendar 1995**
24pp, letterpress with glued in samples, wire binding, 160 x 155, 200 numbered copies, Coracle
**It Was Stuck Up**
126pp, mixed media glued into book, casebound with acrylic, 240 x 170

## 1996

**Special Books by Specialists**
with Simon Cutts, for the New Year 1996
fc, photocopy and rubber stamps

**Italian lesson No.15: Quindici**
pc, 2 colour letterpress, 300 copies, workfortheeyetodo, London
**Italian lesson No.16 : Gnocchi-Gomme**
Boxed eraser, letterpress label, 40 copies, Coracle (*below*)
**Gumigas Zimogs**
64pp, letterpress and rubberstamps, wire binding, 148 x 115, 200 numbered copies, Coracle
**Gumigas Zimogs**
pc for book (several versions)
**Envelope interior card**
pc (green edge)
**Caged Books**
with Simon Cutts, exhibition proposal
16pp, photocopy and rubberstamp, wire binding, Coracle
**Dovecote-fenêtre**
with Simon Cutts
print, lino-cut & letterpress, 340 x 290, 15 signed and numbered copies, Coracle
**Library Doors**
with Simon Cutts, Irish Museum of Modern Art residency
fc, offset
**Remnant Book of Practice Pages for Gumigas Zimogs**
44pp, rubber stamps on paper, buckram over board cover, green spiral binding, 205 x 150
**Remnant Book: I Fingerprinted Italian Lesson No.13**
34pp, fingerprint ink on paper, buckram over card, spiral binding, 195 x 140

## 1997

**Envelope Interior Art History**
with Harry Gilonis
40pp, letterpress album with tipped-in samples, case-bound, slip-case, 150 x 100, 175 numbered copies, Coracle

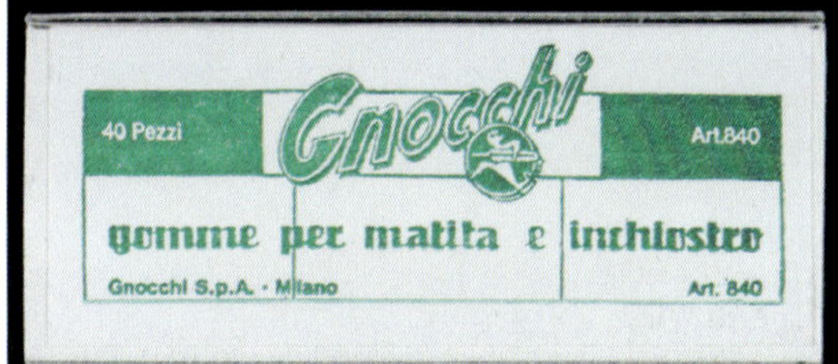


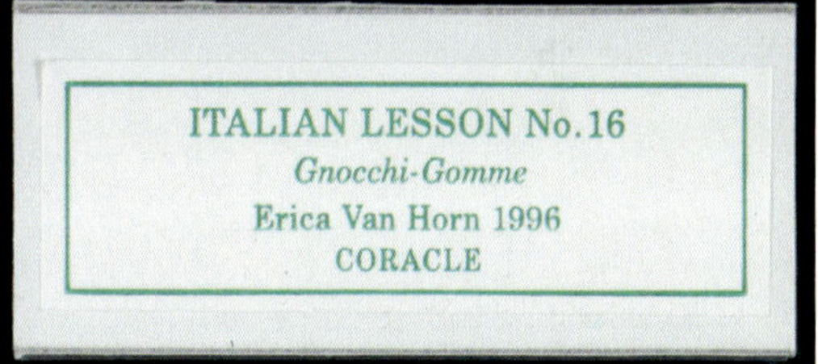

**Envelope Interior Art History**
fc announcement, 160 x 110, letterpress with tip-ins, Coracle
**Envelope Interior Pin-Up Calendar 1997**
24pp, letterpress with tipped-in samples, wire binding, 180 x 180, 200 numbered copies, Coracle
**Envelope Interior Calendar**
pc announcement, letterpress and tip-in, 105 x 135, Coracle
**Industrial Domesticity**
with Simon Cutts
fc, offset, 100 x 150, Coracle
**A Trail of Two Bookshops**
pc, letterpress card to send to people on the walk
**Button Badges** (Envelope interiors)
25 x 25, some in little plastic bags with letterpress card, numbered, 70 x 60
**After Frank O'Hara...**
for the New Year 1997, with Simon Cutts
8pp, letterpress, self-ends over wrappers (wrappers of '00' gauge railway-modeller's crazy paving) with thermographed text, 125 x 110, 200 copies, Coracle

1998

**Fauve Construction**
with Simon Cutts, for the New Year 1998
8pp, with sewn wrapper, laser print, letterpress, Coracle
**A Ventile for Tullio**
with Simon Cutts
fc, 8pp, laser, sewn, 50 copies, Coracle
**A Tree Tie for Odintune Place**
with Simon Cutts
Laminated paper strip with eyelets and string ties, boxed, 270 x 270 x 70, 20 numbered copies, Coracle
**A Trail of Two Bookshops**
with Simon Cutts
Announcement pc for exhibition at Boekie Woekie, Amsterdam, offset
**Remnant Book: Rubber Stamps**
196pp, all available rubber stamps stamped into Italian notebook, one per page, 210 x 155

1999

**14 Blackthorns (a fascicule)**
with Simon Cutts
60pp, letterpress, 2 colours, casebound, 200 x 110, 200 numbered copies, Coracle
**14 Blackthorns**
pc announcement card, 2 colour letterpress, Coracle
**15 Blackthorns**
print, letterpress, 420 x 530, 100 signed and numbered copies, Coracle
**Café Alt Wien**
pc, announcement, letterpress 2 colours, Coracle

**Italian lesson no.17 : Mezzo Marito**
pc, letterpress 2 colours, 300 copies, Coracle
**Envelope interior Pin-up Calendar 1999**
24pp, letterpress with tipped-in samples, wire bound, 160 x 155, 200 numbered copies, Coracle
**World of Interiors**
4pp, information pamphlet in envelope, laser, sewn with wrappers, 150 x 105
**Peanut Butter and Mayonnaise for Jonathan Williams 70th Birthday**
with Simon Cutts, pc, letterpress
**The Pig Poems: Three Poems Concerning Larionov's Provincial Life Series**
with Spike Hawkins
32pp, letterpress in two colours, casebound, 300 x 244, 100 numbered copies, Coracle
**Ambleside Rock**
with Simon Cutts, for the Merzkonferenz
Boxed, mounted candy, letterpress, 120 x 110, 60 numbered copies, Coracle
**Bookmark for Brian Kennedy**
letterpress 2 colours, to accompany *14 Blackthorns* book, 195 x 45
**Stone Wall with painted Coracle**
with Simon Cutts, for the New Year 1999
pc, offset, Coracle

## 2000

**Cuticles Card**
with Simon Cutts, for the New Year 2000
card, letterpress, 140 x 120, 200 copies, Coracle
**Letterpress for Tony Zwicker 1925–2000**
with Simon Cutts
6pp, letterpress and laser, sewn with wrappers, 155 x 150, 50 copies, Coracle
**The Presence of Landscape**
with Simon Cutts, for Limoges exhibition
pc, offset, Centre des Livres d'Artistes, St Yrieix-la-Perche
**Ex Libris for John Janssen**
One of 33 labels, letterpress in multiple colours, 145 x 125, 125 boxed and numbered copies, Coracle
**Pig Poems**
fc, announcement card, photocopy

## 2001

**Nugent's**
for the New Year 2001 with Simon Cutts
laser and letterpress on card, 140 x 120, Coracle
**The Money Jar**
with Simon Cutts
40pp, 4 colour offset with 2 colour interleaving, paper over boards case, 160 x 115, 500 copies, Coracle
**Some Words for Living Locally**
12pp, letterpress in 4 colours, with rubber stamps, finger

print ink and wrappers, 147 x 105, 300 signed and numbered copies, Coracle
**Envelope Interior no.387**
pc, offset, cARTed, Siouville, France

## 2002

**Nearing Arcueil**
with Simon Cutts
32pp, colour offset, sewn wrappers, 170 x 120, 500 copies, Sixtus Editions, Limoges

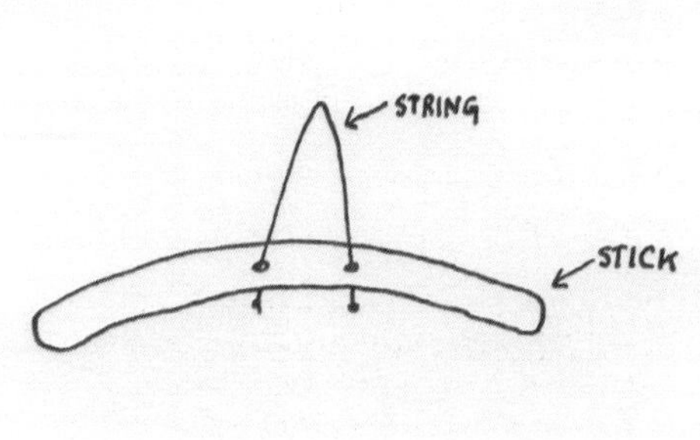


**Airmail Envelope Interiors**
with Simon Cutts
24pp, offset and letterpress with laser, sewn in 2 sections, 115 x 170, 300 numbered copies, Coracle
**The Money Jar & Other recent publications**
with Simon Cutts, announcement card for Coracle exhibition at the Bolton Library, Cashel, Tipperary
pc, letterpress, 165 x 140, Coracle
**Holiday Broadside**
with Simon Cutts, for the New Year 2002
fc, 220 x 140, offset, SUNY Buffalo

## 2003

**Grass Roof**
with Simon Cutts, for the New Year 2003
fc, 105 x 150, laser, 200 copies, Coracle
**Purists Frown on Reading in the Sauna**
with Simon Cutts
plastic plaque with brass fitting pins, in a printed box, 90 x 140, 10 copies, Coracle

## 2004

**MIMO A Story**
32pp, photocopy, 160 x 145, sewn, 30 copies, Coracle
**Envelope Interior Pin-Up Calendar 2004**
24pp, letterpress with tipped-in interiors, wire binding, 180 x 160, 200 numbered copies, Coracle

**Two Peelings**
2 folded cards in wallet, letterpress with glued on examples, (paint peeling & birch bark peeling), 165 x 125, 60 copies, Coracle
**Rusted**
16pp, laser and letterpress in 2 colours, sewn with wrappers, 150 x 105, 100 numbered copies, Coracle
**Shaker hanger**
card, letterpress, 140 x 180, 300 copies *(left)*
**Coracle, New Buildings at Ballybeg 2003**
with Simon Cutts, for the New Year 2004
pc, offset, Coracle

## 2005

**A Bundle of Clothes Pegs**
with Simon Cutts, for the New Year 2005
fc, letterpress with thermography, and hand colouring, 150 x 130, in printed envelope, 300 copies, Coracle
**Queen of Ohio**
(birthday book for Io Worthington at age 10)
22pp, photocopy, sewn, 20 copies
**Tin Pitcher (line drawing)**
fc, laser print, 150 x 105
**Tin Pitcher (solid black)**
fc, laser print, 150 x 105
**Tin Funnel, Jug and Dish**
with Simon Cutts
24pp, laser, letterpress, thermographed image on wrapper, sewn, 200 numbered copies, Coracle
**Favorite Clothes Who Died in France**
pc, offset, Coracle
**Drinking Calendar No.2**
pc. offset, Coracle
**Drinking Calendar No.3**
pc, offset, Coracle
**Chaynie**
pc, letterpress, 300 copies, Coracle
**Our Friend Syd**
with Simon Cutts, memorial card
4pp, laser, sewn wrappers, 35 copies, Coracle *(overleaf)*

## 2006

**Little Red Mugs**
with Simon Cutts, for 2006
fc, laser, 105 x 150, 200 copies, Coracle
**Stilfragen/Tipperary (for Michael Erlhoff at 60)**
pc, letterpress, 300 copies, Coracle
**With My Left Hand (after Les Coleman)**
28pp photocopy with letterpress cover, 165 x 133, 300 stapled copies, 26 copies lettered A–Z and signed with left hand, Coracle

"Our Friend Syd Came Down from the Farm Above Us for the Last Time on Monday November 21st"

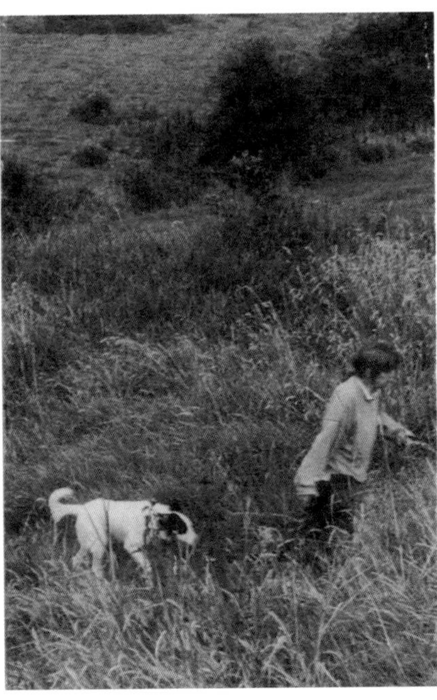

**Led Astray by Language**
with Jonathan Williams, Thomas Meyer, Nancy Kuhl, Richard Deming, Simon Cutts.
24pp offset with letterpress and rubber stamps, sewn into letterpress wrapper, 175 x 135, 300 copies, Coracle
**Folded Napkins**
16pp 2 colour offset with sewn cover wrapper, 150 x 110, 300 numbered copies, Coracle
**Stoppage**
8pp photocopy with letterpress cover, with coloured tip-ins, from the holes cut from Sans Signaux 1990, sewn, 150 x 130, 85 numbered copies, in plastic slipcase, Coracle
**Fourteen Painted Squares in a Cheesebox**
acrylic on 14 pieces of card, 86 x 86, in wooden cheese box 95 x 95 x 25

## 2007

**This card entitles the bearer to one full Irish breakfast**
with Simon Cutts, for the New Year 2007
pc, letterpress, 300 copies, Coracle
**against mice burn sage**
pc, letterpress, 300 copies, Living Locally No.10, Coracle
**Little Critic No.19: The only function of an envelope interior is to hide the contents of the envelope**
16pp, offset, sewn and loose in letterpress cover, 210 x 150, 300 copies, Coracle

**Windscreen Wiper bookmark**
Letterpress and sprayed paint on card, 190 x 60, 100 copies (and proofs)

**Gifts from the Government**
16pp, photocopy with offset, letterpress, laser colour copies, rubber stamps and printed label, sewn cover wrapper, 150 x 110, 300 numbered copies, Living Locally No.11, Coracle

**A Few Cups**
Nine cups, letterpress in Prussian Blue on Bockingford 200lb. cartridge, 250 x 250 each, in blue buckram drop lid box, 25 numbered and signed copies, Coracle

**French Pastry**
Cralan Kelder with printed drawings by Erica Van Horn
8pp, letterpress in 4 colours, on Arches paper, sewn, cover wrappers, 155 x 155, 300 copies, Coracle

**Small Houses: The Buildings of Tom Browne**
48pp, 4-colour offset, casebound, paper over boards, 140 x 170, 500 copies, Living Locally No.12, Coracle

**The Once-A-Year Haircut of Miss Emily Dickinson**
fc, colour laser printed, 30 copies

## 2008

**Eight Old Irish Apples**
with Simon Cutts, for the New Year 2008
8-section concertina, letterpress, 90 x 90, 90 x 720 open, in plastic slip case, 500 copies, Coracle

**Led Astray By Language**
Documents a road trip to visit the poets Jonathan Williams and Thomas Meyer, *Led Astray by Language* includes poems by the writers in Van Horn's company along with the artist's visual and textual record of their days on the road. In addition to facsimile pages of the travel guidebook and notes made during the trip, the volume includes a map of a hotel's emergency exits, small silver reproductions of vanity license plates seen along the way, and bookish images from the illustrated papers covering the windows in an out-of-business bookshop.

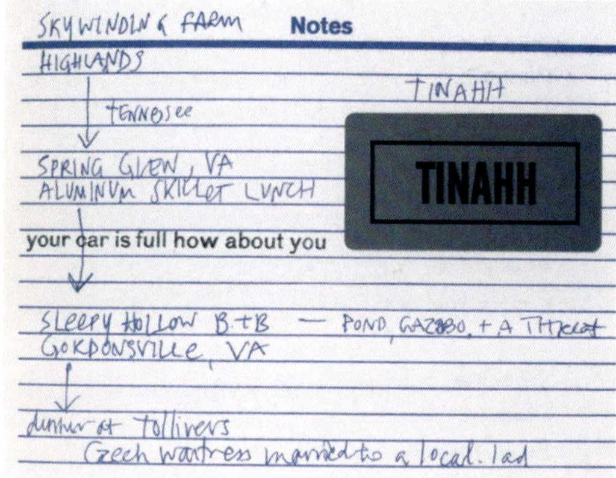

**short-cuts**
with Simon Cutts
8-panel concertina, letterpress, 150 x 90, in acetate sleeve, 300 copies, Coracle
**An Album of Interiors**
36pp letterpress with fifteen tipped-in samples of envelope interiors, casebound, 235 x 170, 175 numbered copies
**Forty Fungi**
poems by Harry Gilonis
96pp offset with letterpress cover, second edition of 1994 book with one additional poem, sewn paperback, 175 x 130, 300 copies, Coracle
**A Rosemary Copybook**
80pp, ink and coloured pencil, papercovers, 140 x 100
**Rusted**
16pp, laser and letterpress in 2 colours, sewn with wrappers, 150 x 105. Second edition 150 numbered copies, Coracle
**Recently Read**
6pp, acrylic and letterpress on watercolour paper, glued into casebinding, buckram over boards with laser images, 220 x 125

*(below)* Windscreen Wiper bookmark

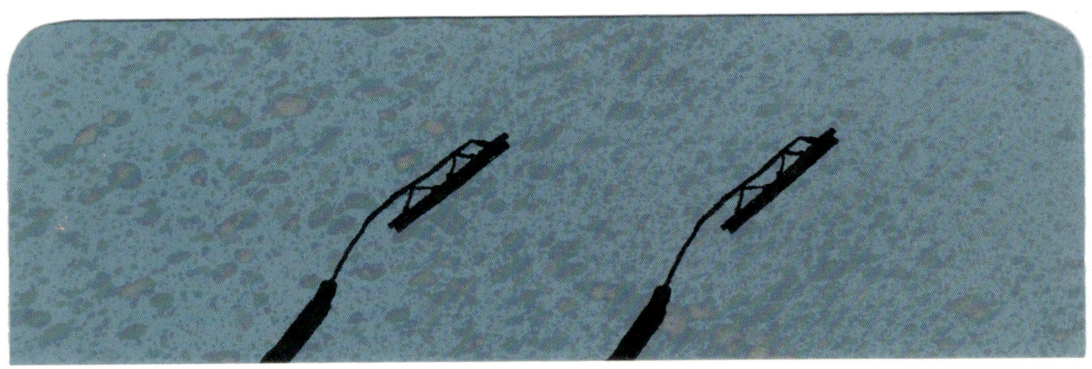

## 2009

**Rosemary**
enamel plaque, 215 x 125, boxed, 10 copies, Coracle

**Kintsugi**
drawings for a poem by Thomas Meyer
24pp, letterpress, sewn, paper covers, 100 copies, 220 x 155, Punch Press

**Living Locally No.16: Rain**
pc, acrylic and letterpress, 300 copies

**Wildflower for Deidre**
with Simon Cutts
4pp, photocopy and laser, sewn in paper cover, 200 x 85

**Silk Worm Box**
12pp, laser with silk paper insert, sewn self-cover, in plastic sleeve, 175 copies, Coracle

**Return from New York May 2009**
with Simon Cutts, for the New Year 2010
pc, offset, 200 copies, Coracle

**Nine Views of Ballybeg (in a cheesebox.) August 2009**
9 pieces, acrylic on 6mm plywood, 115 x 115, wooden cheese box 130 x 130 x 65 (*right*)

**Nine Views of Ballybeg in a Cheesebox August 2009**
9 pieces, acrylic on marine plywood, 55 x 110, wooden cheese box with ribbon, 65 x 120 x 30

**Copybook: The Book Remembers Everything**
80pp, ink and coloured pencil, paper wrapper, 140 x 100

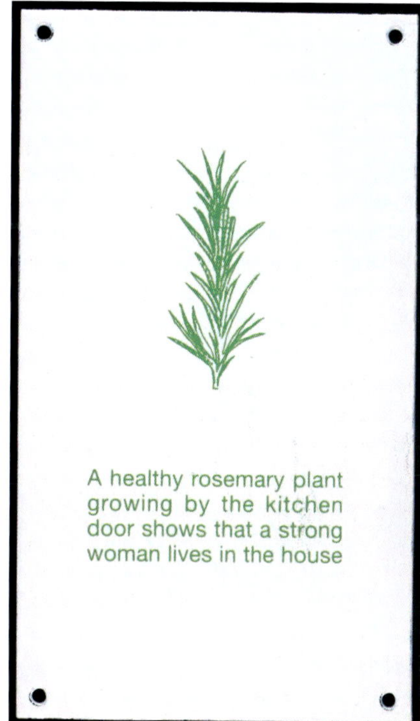

## Acknowledgements

Grateful acknowledgement is made to the Beinecke Rare Book and Manuscript Library for use of images from the Yale Collection of American Literature; special thanks are due to Director Frank Turner and the staff of the Library's Digital Studio.

All quotations of Erica Van Horn in *The Book Remembers Everything* are from her books or from personal correspondence with Nancy Kuhl.

The photograph of the de-installation at Aichi University Museum in 2008 is by Shinya Aota.

g. The book. The book remembers everything. The book remem
emembers everything. The book remembers everything. The book r
ything. The book remembers everything. The book. The book. The
ook remembers. The book remembers everything. The book rememb
everything. The book remembers everything. The book remembers
members everything. The book remembers everything. The book reme
. The book remembers everything. The book remembers everythin
mbers everything. The book. The book. The book remembers. T
s everything. The book remembers everything. The book remem
The book remembers everything. The book remembers everything. The
ers everything. The book remembers. The book remembers. The book rem
ng. The book remembers everything. The book. The book remembers ever
nembers everything. The book remembers everything. The book remem
verything. everything. The book remembers everything. The book re
ers everything. The book remembers everything. The book rememb
The book remembers everything. The book remembers everything
members everything. The book remembers everything. The book r